INNS
and their
SIGNS
FACT
& FICTION

Eric R Delderfield

DAVID & CHARLES
Newton Abbot · London
North Pomfret (Vt) · Vancouver

By the same author

British Inn Signs and their Stories
Church Furniture
Eric Delderfield's Book of True Animal Stories (two volumes)
Introduction to Inn Signs
Kings and Queens of England and Great Britain
Stories of Inns and their Signs
West Country Historic Houses and their Families (three volumes)

ISBN 0 7153 7112 6

Library of Congress Catalog Card Number 75-10564

Printed in Great Britain
by Ebenezer Baylis & Son Ltd
for David & Charles (Holdings) Limited
Brunel House Newton Abbot Devon

Published in the United States of America
by David & Charles Inc
North Pomfret Vermot 05053 USA

Published in Canada
by Douglas David & Charles Limited
1875 Welch Street North Vancouver BC

Introduction

This book presents in alphabetical form some hundreds of names of inns, thus making possible quick and easy reference. It explains as far as is practicable how the names were derived and gives information on some interesting inn signs.

The subject is full of interest, vast in its scope and continually fluid. Old names are being discarded for new ones; inns which have been a meeting place for generations are being demolished for road improvements, taking with them the delightful atmosphere which can never be recaptured with a new building. New inns are being erected, but alas they are so often 'chromium-plated palaces'.

It is amazing just how much of Britain's history is recalled and reflected by inns and their signs. Older generations do not need reminding of the fame and accomplishments of Lloyd George or W. G. Grace, but recently a lad of fourteen who had never heard of either was well-informed about Hitler and Nazi Germany. This will go some way to explain why many old signs which are self-explanatory to some of us have been included. It is also a good reason for resisting a change of name for an old-established inn without very good reason.

Through inn signs even the casual observer can learn a great deal, for they commemorate the curious as at *Old Parr's Head* or *Henry Jenkins*; they perpetuate the fame of giants and freaks as at *Childe of Hale* or *Daniel Lambert*; they help to educate us about foreign personalities who have in the past done great service for Britain, such as *Angerstein*, *Von Alten* or *Vermuyden*.

The most ancient inns were originally hostels erected for pilgrims and bore religious titles. Still surviving are *Salutation*, *Star* and *Seven Stars*, *St Peter's Finger* and a number of others.

Great victories which gave our forebears immense satisfaction received the accolade of an inn sign and may now only rarely be recalled in any other way: *Moodkee*, *Minden Rose*, *Aliwal*, *Odessa*, *Gibraltar*, *Balaclava*, *Inkerman*, *Alma* and *Sebastapol*.

Not everyone will appreciate that the *Daylight* inn recalls the Daylight Saving Bill instigated by William Willet in 1916; that Isambard Brunel had a hand in a great but unsuccessful railway experiment which is recalled by the sign of the *Atmospheric Railway* inn. The sign of the *Bridge* at Yatton, Somerset, carries a quaint mechanical design on its sign—why? The *Turbinia* features another invention. Television is part of our way of life but it takes an inn sign to remind many that John Baird was its inventor in 1926. The Belisha beacon is familiar to all, but there will be many who would like more factual information. There is a *Crutched Friar*, a *Blackfriars* and an *Antigallican*—why?

Every Scot will know the meaning of the inn called *1314* but few Englishmen will be able to hazard a guess.

We are reminded of notorious characters, too, by the inns named to recall the exploits of Dick Turpin, Jacob Harris, or Cannard. Soothsayers are represented by *Mother Shipton* and *Old Mother Redcap*, and eccentrics like Old Job, Castleton and Monolulu have inns named after them. There are inns named *Dog Tray*, *Karrozzin*, *Doffcocker*, *Harnser*, *Wig & Fidgett*, *Sun & 13 Cantons*, *Cat i' the Window*, and they all have a meaning.

What is the derivation of the *Bay & Say*, *Tinker's Budget*, *Spinner & Bergamot*, *Magpie & Stump*, *Clog & Billycock*, *Cornkist*, *Tontine* and *Letter B*? The list of intriguing names is endless.

Undoubtedly some of the most fascinating are those recalling old or unusual trades and callings. Not everyone knows the occupation of a huffler, flint knapper, scutcher, clicker, coulter, slubber, higgler or jugg. But the inns named to attract the custom of these men still exist, and in some cases so do the trades. Some inns were named after the tools of the trade such as *Bettel & Chisel*, *Bushel & Strike* or *Beetle & Wedge*.

Famous people past and present provide an enormous list of inn names and signs, and the brief notes against these entries will, I hope, add to the interest and usefulness of the book. They extend over a wide field and include William Wilberforce, Louis Kossuth, Sir Joseph Paxton, Samuel Pepys, Jenny Lind, Bob Fitzsimmons, Friar Bacon, Miles Coverdale, John Bunyan, Richard Cobden, William Caxton and Tom Cribb.

Innkeepers and brewery companies are keeping us up-to-date with history. Apart from the spate of space-travel signs there is the *Lone Yachtsman*; *Concorde* is represented by the *Double-o-Two*, Giles the great cartoonist has his sign, a *New Penny* marks the advent of decimal coinage, but tradition is not entirely forgotten for there is also a *Half Crown*. Even the mundane *Park* is enlivened by a sign depicting the robot which is so much a part of our lives today—a parking meter. Esperanto has its niche for there is a *Green Star*, symbol of the society in Staffordshire.

For the purposes of this book every house has been deemed an inn which has an honoured tradition of hospitality. Where a town or place has been inserted after the name it is with some degree of certainty and to the best of my knowledge the only one; where no locality appears there are at least two inns with the name.

It is of course obvious that most names are either preceded by 'the' or followed by 'arms' or 'inn'. These do not appear in the text. Every care has been taken with detail, and if despite this errors do occur, sincere apologies are offered.

Finally my grateful thanks to a number of indefatigable correspondents who keep me informed of closures and changes of names, in their own districts. They also communicate new and strange names which I can follow up. Letters and enquiries come from all over the world and I am always as pleased to help with them as to receive information. Typical is the letter which arrived from a remote part of Australia to ask if 'a pub—my grandfather's favourite—is still going strong in the Old Kent Road?'

Librarians and their staffs all over Britain are my especial friends, for they can delve into the past more efficiently than most licensees, and funnily enough they also seem to care more. To the brewers and their signboard artists I also accord my thanks.

I should add that humorous signs have no place in this book, but there is always an exception. I award pride of place to the *Jolly Taxpayer*, even if it does call for a fertile imagination.

E.R.D.

Exmouth, March 1975

Adam & Eve Originally a religious sign there are still many such to be found. The Fruiterers Company adopted Adam and Eve for their arms but the sign was popular long before.

Admiral Codrington (London SW3) Sir Edward Codrington (1770-1851) commanded a ship at Trafalgar and had a distinguished naval career.

Admiral Duncan (London W1) Recalls Adam Duncan (1731-1804) whose successful career was crowned by his victory at Camperdown in 1797.

Admiral Hardy Named after Sir Thomas Hardy, Flag Captain to Lord Nelson in the *Victory* at Trafalgar. Was first sea lord and later Governor of Greenwich hospital.

Admiral Harvey Takes the name of Sir Eliab Harvey (1758-1830) who commanded the *Temeraire* at Trafalgar. Was known as a reckless gambler.

Admiral Hawke (Boston Spa, Yorks) The sign has a portrait of the Admiral in full regalia at this Samuel Smith house. Edward Hawke, first Baron Hawke (1705-81), went to sea as a volunteer at the age of fourteen and had a brilliant career. He was ahead of his time in concern for the health of his men. Created a peer 1776. His mother's family had Yorkshire roots which accounts for the name of the inn at Boston.

Admiral Keppel Honours Augustus, 1st Viscount Keppel (1725-86) who accompanied Anson on a voyage round the world in 1740.

Admiral Macbride (Plymouth, Devon) Honours the man who had a successful naval career and was MP for Plymouth.

Air Balloon Several are thought to commemorate the space race at Versailles 200 years ago. During the siege of Paris in 1871, 54 balloons were despatched carrying $2\frac{1}{2}$ million letters—an event which possibly caught the imagination of the innkeepers. The balloon was invented by Montgolfier (1745-99), the first ascent being made in 1783.

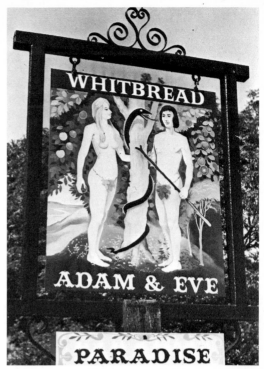

Paradise, Gloucestershire

Exmouth, Devon

Albert Edward (Eccles, Manchester) An unusual title for an inn named after a monarch. The sign shows Edward VII in cameo.

Alice Hawthorn The name of a famous racehorse, bred at Wheldrake (Yorks), which became a legend. She ran 71 times and won 51 races outright, was placed 10 times and once ran a dead-heat. In the period 1842-45 the horse won 16 cups including the Chester, Doncaster, and Goodwood and 18 Queen's Plates. Racing days finished, she became one of the greatest brood mares in history.

Alma There are many of these which commemorate the Allied victory over the Russians in the Crimean War, 1854. The Alma was the river which the French and British crossed to attack.

Altisdora A racehorse owned by a local squire at Bishop Burton (Yorks). The local innkeeper staked all he had on the horse in the St Leger in 1813, it won the race and the inn was promptly named after the horse in gratitude.

Anchor Originally a religious sign, indicating that it was the Christian faith which kept men safe from the storms of life. This sign is to be found not only in seaports, but in places completely unconnected with water.

Angel & Royal (Grantham, Lincs) An ancient inn, probably thirteenth century, with a rich history—many monarchs have stayed there. It received the Royal accolade after a visit by the Prince of Wales (later Edward VII). An intriguing fact is that, when the landlord died in 1707, he left a legacy of 40 shillings a year for a sermon to be preached annually about the evils of drunkenness. The payment is still made and the sermon still preached.

Angerstein (Greenwich, London) John Julius Angerstein (1735-1823) is considered the father of Lloyds of London. He was largely responsible for the abandonment of the original Lloyds Coffee House and founded the present institution. Of Russian extraction, he first came to London when fifteen. By the time he was twenty-one, he was an under-

Bass Charrington

Anchor

Eling, Hampshire

WHITBREAD

ANGEL & CROWN

Islington, London

writer and soon became an important figure in the commercial world. He was a merchant, philanthropist and an amateur collector of fine art. With Sir Thomas Lawrence he acquired during his lifetime a collection of pictures which, on his death, were purchased for £60,000 and formed the nucleus of the National Gallery. Many of the Gallery's richest treasures came from the collection.

Antigallican (Charlton, London) Name came from a British warship built in 1771 which served in the Napoleonic wars. Gallican referred to Gaul, the Roman name for France. In 1757 an Anti-Gallican Society was formed in London with the object of promoting English commerce and discouraging that of France.

Arabian Horse (Aberford, Yorks) It is suggested that it comes from the great Arab thoroughbred stallion Godolphin, from which all famous racehorses are descended.

Argus (Peterloo, Co Durham) Named after the butterfly.

Arroyo (Carlisle, Cumbria) One of many names which commemorates the battle of Arroyo dos Molinos, fought in the Peninsular War in 1811. The Border Regiment played a prominent part in the victory; a drummer boy is shown on the sign.

Atmospheric Railway (Starcross, Devon) In 1836 the great engineer, Isambard Kingdom Brunel, built an extraordinary railway system for the Great Western Railway on the western side of the river Exe; the system ran on air pressure built up in 15in cast-iron pipes to provide traction for the train. It was never a success and had a very short life. The inn is situated near the site of part of the experiment.

Auld Lang Syne (Oldham, Lancs) Named after the title of the song by Robert Burns, Scottish National poet.

Axe & Compass A typical trade sign which is often seen. The sign usually represents the arms of the Company of Carpenters.

Bacchanales This was the original name taken from the triennial festivals held in Rome in honour of the god of wine. It was corrupted to 'Bag o' Nails', and several inns are so named.

Bacchus A natural and popular inn name; Bacchus was the god of wine in Roman mythology. He was early represented as a bearded man, later a handsome youth, with a chariot drawn by panthers. The famous statue in Rome depicts him holding a bunch of grapes with a panther at his feet. The name is a corruption of *Iacchus* (Greek) from *Iache*, a shout. He was originally thought of as a rowdy god.

Bailiff's Sergeant (St Mary's Bay, Kent) Named after the official who for hundreds of years served the Lords Bailiffs and Jurats of Romney Marsh, the body responsible for the maintenance of flood protection and preventative works on the marshes.

Balaclava Recalls the battle (1854) during the Crimean War, in which the British cavalry distinguished itself by two astonishing charges against overwhelming odds. The second charge has gone down in history as the Charge of the Light Brigade. Through a blunder of unparalleled stupidity, the courage of the 673 horsemen involved caught the imagination of the British public, resulting in many inns being named after the battle. The episode is immortalised in verse by Tennyson's *Charge of the Light Brigade*.

Balancing Eel (South Shields, Tyne & Wear) The inspiration for the name came from a verse in *Alice in Wonderland*. The sign depicts a mariner holding on to a rope with an eel balanced on his nose:

> Yet you balanced an eel on the end
> of your nose,
> What made you so awfully clever?

Bank of England (Ancoats, Lancs) Nothing official about the name, merely a compliment to a former landlord who in his dealings was deemed 'as safe as the Bank of England'.

Barnaby Rudge (Broadstairs, Kent) Named after the character in Charles Dickens' famous novel which dealt with the Gordon riots. Published in 1841, it was an immediate success.

Bathpool (Bathpool, Som) The sign shows a display of the local volunteer forces at the period when the Spanish Armada invasion was expected. The muster parades were in fact held on the green outside the inn.

Battle (Reading, Berks) Takes its name from the nearby Battle hospital, so called because of a medieval connection with Battle Abbey.

Battle of Britain Several inns have been so renamed since 1945, particularly in Kent which bore much of the brunt of the prolonged aerial operations in August and September, 1940, when the German Luftwaffe failed to gain air superiority as a necessary prelude to invasion.

Battledown (Cheltenham, Glos) Recalls that a skirmish between Cavaliers and Roundheads took place in the area.

Bay & Say (Colchester, Essex) Named after two basic types of cloth, bay being used chiefly for garments and say, a coarser, tougher material for blankets, etc. The inn was so christened as Flemish weavers fleeing from persecution in the sixteenth century left Europe to settle in Colchester, where a Dutch quarter grew up. The sign shows a man and woman in sixteenth-century costume, each with a bolt of cloth under their arm. See *Flemish Weaver*.

Beaconsfield There are many inns which recall Benjamin Disraeli (1804-81) who became Earl of Beaconsfield in 1876. He introduced and carried through the Reform Bill of 1875 and it was due to his far-sightedness that Britain secured half the shares of the Suez Canal. He was twice Prime Minister and also wrote several novels. The signs vary from *Beaconsfield Arms* to *Earl of Beaconsfield*.

Bear Quite numerous, many dating from the days when bears were baited as a 'sport'—

Bathpool, Somerset

Bishops Frome, Herefordshire

Sir Hugh Walpole described it in *Judith Paris*. It was not so prevalent as bull-baiting. Some *Bear* signs stem from heraldic crests or coats of arms.

Bear & Billet (Chester, Ches) A variation on the *Bear & Ragged Staff*.

Bear & Ragged Staff Comes from the crest of the Earls of Warwick, a forebear of whom was named Arthal, signifying a bear. After him came Morvidus, who slew a giant with a young ash tree which he tore up by the roots. From this came the ragged staff, which became a sign on his shield. Thus the bear and ragged staff has been the crest of the Earls of Warwick for centuries and the sign is frequently seen. See also *Dun Cow, Bear & Billet*.

Beefeater (Bishops Frome, Herefs) History and tradition go hand-in-hand on the sign which shows a beefeater or yeoman of the guard. The body was founded by Henry VII in 1485. The term 'eater' was formerly used as a synonym for servant.

Beetle & Wedge (Moulsford, Berks) Refers to a beetle—a heavy wooden mallet used with a wedge for splitting logs. See also *Bettle & Chisel*.

Belisha Beacon (Gillingham, Kent) So quickly do origins become faded that possibly many people do not recall that the beacons at pedestrian crossings were named after Leslie Hore-Belisha (1893-1957) the Member of Parliament who, as Minister of Transport, was responsible for their appearance in 1934, together with the Highway Code and driving tests for motorists.

Bell A very popular sign in a variety of forms, which demonstrates the Englishman's love of bells. Sometimes situated near the parish church or cathedral. A variety of four, five, eight and even twelve bells; makes up hundreds of signs over the country. Sometimes handbells, still a popular form of ringing, are pictured on the sign, in villages in particular. There are some forty thousand people who are enthusiastic ringers in the British Isles. See also *Ring o' Bells*.

Bass

Barley Mow

Gloucester

WHITBREAD

THE BASKETMAKERS

Littlebourne, Kent

Bell & Hare (Tottenham, London) The sign of a hare jumping clear of a bell, book and candle, is a reminder of the legend that witches transformed themselves into hares, their only defence against excommunication.

Ben Jonson (Wigan, Lancs) English dramatist and poet who was a friend of Shakespeare and Bacon.

Berkeley Many inns in the Westcountry refer to the family of the name. An exception is that at Burton-on-Trent (Staffs) where it has a local meaning, a 'berkeley' being a clearing in a wood.

Bettel & Chisel (Delabole, Cornwall) 'Bettel' is just a mispronunciation of beetle. Probably the two tools were used in the slate industry for which this part of Cornwall is famous. See also *Beetle & Wedge*.

Bible & Crown The words were a favourite toast of the Royalists during the Civil War. The sign was popular in the beginning of the troubles but most of them disappeared when it became foolhardy to be partisan.

Biddy Mulligan (Kilburn, London) The name of the inn was changed as a compliment to the large Irish population in the area.

Big Lock The inn takes its name from the lock, part of the Chester Canal which was built 1772. The connection from Nantwich to Middlewich was not proceeded with until the 1820s.

Bird in Hand Its origin probably stemmed from the sport of falconry. Some have been taken from coats of arms, and a more facetious meaning comes from the proverb 'a bird in the hand is worth two in the bush', the bush in this case being a rival inn. See also *Falcon*.

Bishop & Wolf (Isles of Scilly, Cornwall) Refers to the two famous lighthouses, Wolf Rock and Bishop Rock. The latter occupies one of the most exposed positions of any lighthouse in the world and stands 163 ft high. The Wolf Rock light is 135 ft high.

WHITBREAD

The Black Boy

Killay, Glamorgan

Bishop Blaise A popular sign particularly in the north country, as he was the patron saint of woolcombers. His symbol is iron combs, with which his body was torn to pieces. A particularly fine sign is at the *Bishop Blaise*, Richmond, Yorks, which in the reign of Elizabeth was a centre for wool distribution.

Bishop Lacy (Chudleigh, Devon) Named after the eminent fifteenth-century prelate who was Bishop of Exeter (1370-1455).

Black Boy (Killay, Glam) A fine sign shows a smiling black boy. In the seventeenth and eighteenth centuries they were greatly in demand as personal attendants.

Black Cap Usually the sign depicts a witch on a broomstick.

Black Friar (Queen Victoria St, London) In medieval times a monastery of the Dominican order stood in the vicinity, from which the name of the district originated. The brothers known as the Black Friars from the colour of their habits, came to London and set up a priory where Lincoln's Inn now stands. Later they moved to what is now Printing House Square. Elsewhere in London is the *Monks Tavern*, also associated by name with the Black Friars. See also *Crutched Friar*.

Black Lion Stemmed from a noble's coat of arms. The black variety is one of more than a score of various types and coloured lions from *Rampant Lion* to *Lion & Snake* and *Whyte Lion*. See also *Lion*.

Black Prince Named after Edward, Prince of Wales (1330-76) eldest son of Edward III. Said to have acquired the title by reason of his black armour, but there is no official record of this. He fought at the battle of Crecy when sixteen years old. Buried in Canterbury Cathedral where his surcoat, helmet, shield and gauntlets are still preserved.

Black Venus (Challacombe, Devon) A free house, it carried this name until 1824, when it was changed to *Ring o' Bells*. In recent years the proprietor discovered that black venus was a name given to a black sheep found occasionally in the flocks of this extensive sheep country, and thinking it most appropriate, reverted to the original name.

Blackamoor's Head One of a series which came from crusading times, when any coloured man was rated an infidel and automatically barbarous and cruel. See also *Turk's Head, Saracen's Head*, etc.

Bladebone (Bucklebury Common, Berks) The inn was so named following the discovery nearby of a large bone of a prehistoric monster.

Bladud (Bath, Som) Named after the mythical king of England and father of King Lear. He built the city of Bath and dedicated the medicinal springs to Minerva.

Bleeding Horse The sign shows the head of a horse with what appear to be drops of blood on its neck. Originally heraldic the 'spots' were of ermine, but through lack of

Ongar, Sussex

knowledge the ermine was portrayed as blood—hence the name.

Blue Backs (Warrington, Lancs) The only one of this name in the country. It was the nickname of the Loyal Warrington Volunteers. Formed at the end of the eighteenth century at the time of the threatened Napoleonic invasion, the regiment was disbanded in 1801 but continued to use the inn as an unofficial 'headquarters' for many years.

Blue Ball Still fairly numerous, it was always popular as the sign of a fortune teller.

Blue Boar A popular sign as it was the badge of the House of York. It was also the badge of the de Vere's, Earls of Oxford. See also *White Boar*.

Blue Bowl Not an uncommon name in the Bristol/Bath area where there are associations with the manufacturers of Bristol ware. The bowls were traditionally associated with punch.

Blue Boy There are several of the name and most signs, as that at Clapton, Somerset, have a painting after Gainsborough's famous picture.

Brecon, Monmouth

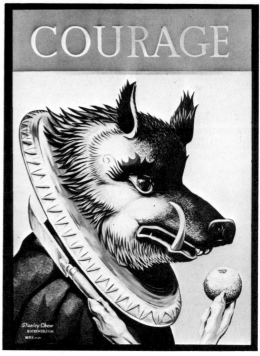

Boar's Head, Aust, Gloucestershire

Clapton, Somerset

Blue Boys (Tonbridge, Kent) Name originated from a halt at the inn by the coach of George IV. His postillions wore a blue livery.

Blue Lias (Stockton, Tyne & Wear) Named after the limestone hewn in the vicinity, which was transported by barge along the local canal.

Blue Vinny (Puddletown, Dorset) From the Dorsetshire 'blue veiny' cheese, so-called because of its blue-veined appearance. See also *Double Gloucester*.

Bluebird (Plymouth, Devon) The sign shows the famous racing car in which Sir Malcolm Campbell captured the world land-speed record in 1935: he was the first to exceed 300 mph.

Bob Fitzsimmons (Helston, Cornwall) It is fitting that R. J. Fitzsimmons (1862-1917) should be honoured by an inn sign, for he was born at Helston though he grew up in New Zealand. He won the world middleweight boxing championship at New Orleans in 1891, and the world heavyweight championship from Jim Corbett in 1897.

Bombay Grab (Bow Road, London) A 'ghrab' was an Indian native-built vessel with two or three masts and in design a mixture of early nineteenth-century naval architecture and a dhow. Such boats were used by the Honourable East India Company. It was the transport of ale from Bow brewery to Bombay for the troops which led to the naming of the inn and at the same time to making the introduction of East India pale ale, the first consignment of which was despatched in 1734.

Boot Inns named *Boot* or *Shoe* are more numerous than any recording other items of apparel. *Boot* is a common sign, probably stemming from the thirsty reputation of cobblers. It is particularly popular for another reason in Bedfordshire, Buckinghamshire and Huntingdonshire, where it commemorates a legendary monk, John Schorne, who is said to have conjured the devil into a boot at a time of great drought, thereby ending the calamity. The *Boot* in Grays Inn Road, London, was mentioned by Charles Dickens in a novel.

Bounty (Maryport, Cumbria) Named to commemorate the mutiny on the *Bounty*, 1798. Fletcher Christian, who led the mutiny, was born at Moorland Close, a farmhouse in the nearby town of Cockermouth.

Brentor (Brentor, Devon) This famous Dartmoor tor is an isolated cone of volcanic rock rising 1130ft. On the summit is the thirteenth-century church of St Michael which is shown on the sign.

Bridge (Yatton, Som) The sign shows a fascinating contraption known in 1850, when it was invented, as an 'Impulsoria'. It was one of the odd inventions which followed the railway frenzy of the mid-nineteenth century. A pair of large wheels, a chain drive, and a pair of horses were the means of supplying animal power to supersede the costly locomotive.

Bridgewater (Stockport, Ches) Commemorates the Duke of Bridgewater (1736-1803) 'father' of British canals. He built the earliest canal in England uniting Worsley

WHITBREAD

THE BOOT

Lapworth, Warwickshire

WHITBREAD

BRENTOR

Brentor, Devon

with Manchester; 42 miles long, it was the brainchild of James Brindley, who though illiterate was responsible for planning and building 365 miles of canals.

Bridgwater Squib (Bridgwater, Som) Named in association with the annual carnival held in November, when there are amazing jollifications in connection with Guy Fawkes.

Brigadier (Nr Manchester) Named after the famous racehorse, Brigadier Gerard; the horse was retired to stud in 1973 having been beaten only once in eighteen races and then by the 1972 Derby winner Roberto. The streets surrounding the inn are named after various racecourses.

British Oak (Bowbridge, Glos) Shows an oak tree surmounted by a British flag and recalls the part played by British grown oak trees in the history of this island. In the closing days of the eighteenth century thousands of oak trees went into the building of each ship which fought for, gained and maintained British sea supremacy.

Brittania There are many inns bearing the name and commemorating a variety of things. At Camden Town, London, the sign recalls the author, William Camden, who in 1586 published in latin his famous *Brittania— A Survey of the British Isles*. At Nailsworth (Glos) the sign illustrates a ship's figurehead, while at Elterwater (Cumbria) the 100-gun warship which entered the Royal Navy in 1682 is shown. An aircraft—the Brittania— is depicted on the sign of the inn at Dover (Kent). See also *William Camden*.

Brown Derby (Birmingham) The theme of the inn is the theatrical world of the 1920s.

Buckle (Seaford, Sussex) Associated with a local family, the Pelhams. In the French wars at the time of Edward III, Sir John Pelham is said to have captured the French king by seizing the buckle of his belt. Henceforth he was allowed to incorporate a buckle in his coat of arms.

Bugle (Hamble, Hants) One of the oldest inns in Hampshire with a history dating back

Bridgwater, Somerset

Near Manchester

to the twelfth century, it is believed to have derived from the ancient bugle or bull's horn.

Bull A very popular name and sign. In the earliest days this was a religious sign derived from La Boule (latin *bulla*) the seal of a collegiate body or monastery. Later the *Bull* became popular all over the British Isles due largely to the horrible bull-baiting so popular in Tudor and Stuart England, and not in fact prohibited by law until 1835. The animal was tethered to an iron ring set in the ground and specially trained dogs were set upon it. There is a *Bull* in almost every market town and at Brading (Isle of Wight) the ring is still in place.

Bull in Spectacles (Nr Lichfield, Staffs) The name is derived from the comment of a local wag who, when a bull almost died from eating poisonous berries, suggested the beast should be fitted with spectacles to avoid further trouble.

Buller There are several signs to honour Sir Redvers Buller (1839-1908) in his native Westcountry. Served in the Chinese, Ashanti, Kaffir and Zulu wars, in the last of which he won the VC. He also served in the Egyptian war and the Sudan expedition. Commander-in-Chief at the Boer War, where he raised the siege of Ladysmith. He was very popular with the British public.

Bullnose Morris (Oxford, Oxon) Some forty years after production of the famous car of the name ceased, an inn was named in its honour.

Bunch of Carrots (Hampton Bishop, Herefs) Takes its name from a rock formation in the river Wye on the banks of which the inn is situated.

Bunker's Knob (Addington, Surrey) The name comes in a tortuous way from a local worthy, William Coppin, who lived in the 1850s. He was parish constable and clerk and in addition looked after the pitch of Addington cricket club (founded 1743). He had a club foot which produced the nickname 'Bunker' and the knob came from the nearby Great Castle hill, where he used to while away his time.

WHITBREAD

BRICKLAYER'S ARMS

Westmorland Road, London

WHITBREAD

BULL & BUTCHER

Bridgwater, Somerset

Bunter (Bromley Common, Kent) Formerly the *Crown* but recently renamed in honour of Billy Bunter, the fictional fat boy (the inspiration of Frank Richards) who appeared in the boys' paper, the *Magnet*.

Burdett Takes the name from Sir Francis Burdett (1770-1844). Popular politician. When the House of Commons imprisoned a radical orator, he declared it had done so illegally and was sent to the Tower. He later married the philanthropist Baroness Burdett-Coutts.

Busby Stoop (Nr Thirsk, Yorks) Named after a murderer who was hung in chains on the nearby gibbet some 300 years ago.

Bush One of the earliest of signs, for as far back as Roman times bunches of evergreens fixed to a pole indicated a wine shop. From this came the phrase 'a good wine needs no bush'. Later, the sign was used for ale houses. Later still a garland displayed outside an inn meant a new brew, a custom still followed in some places.

Bushel & Strike The strike still survives as a measure in some ports. It is a 'struck' bushel—the measure being filled level to the brim only, any surplus being removed with a rod, as contrasting with a 'heaped' bushel. Possibly emanated from a trade sign of the cornchandlers.

Bustard Named after a bird the size of a turkey which has been extinct in Britain since 1840. One of its last habitats was Salisbury Plain, where attempts are now being made to reintroduce it.

Byron House (Bristol, Glos) The name is a compliment to George Gordon Byron (1788-1824) the poet.

Cadland (Chilwell, Notts) This was a famous racehorse owned by the Duke of Rutland in 1828. It ran a dead-heat with The Colonel in the Derby of 1828; on the re-run, Cadland won by a neck. See also *Running Horses*.

Rochester, Kent

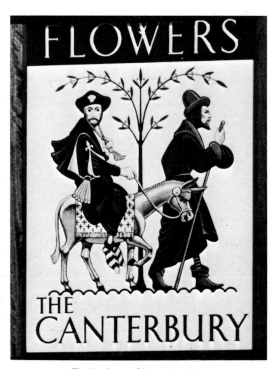

Tewkesbury, Gloucestershire

Cannards Grave (Nr Shepton Mallet, Som) Has a macabre sign portraying a man hanging from a gibbet. This was Cannard, who was not only an innkeeper but also 'out of hours' a highwayman. Reputed to be the last man in England hanged for such a crime, he was buried at the crossroads, a usual practice where felons were concerned, as no parish was anxious to have them buried within its boundaries.

Canopus (Rochester, Kent) A reminder of the great Empire flying-boat launched at Rochester in 1936 which covered well over two million miles in its lifetime.

Captain Cook (Barking, Essex) James Cook (1728-79) the labourer's son who, starting as a common seaman in the navy, had a distinguished naval career. Made several antarctic voyages. In 1777-9 he endeavoured to discover a passage round the north coast of America from the Pacific. He was murdered by natives in Hawaii.

Captain Webb (Wellington, Salop) Named after Captain Matthew Webb (1849-83), a captain in the Mercantile Marine who, in 1875, became the first man to swim the English Channel, which he accomplished in 22 hours, swimming 40 miles. Died attempting to swim the rapids at Niagara Falls.

Cardinal (Hampton Court, Middx) After Thomas Wolsey (1475-1530) the English cardinal who rose to great heights as a minister of Henry VIII, but became unpopular over the king's divorce from Anne Boleyn. He built Hampton Court Palace for himself but made it a gift to the king. See also *Cardinal's Error*.

Cardinal's Error (Tonbridge, Kent) A reminder that the great and all powerful Cardinal Wolsey suppressed Tonbridge priory. He promised to build a great grammar school in its place but fell from favour before he could accomplish it—the Cardinal's error. See also *Cardinal*.

Caribou (Glasson, Lancs) So named because of the local association with the Canadian trade. It is also said that caribou is an old country name for a badger.

Case is Altered The true meaning is lost in antiquity—there are at least three versions. At Woodbridge (Suffolk) the inn of the name stands on the site of an ancient nunnery which Father Casey used to visit for confessions. After the Reformation, an inn was built on the site and a garbled version of Casey's altar became 'the Case is altered'. From Harrow (Middx) comes a different story. The inn was patronised by soldiers of the 57th Regiment of Foot (later the Middlesex Regiment) who had recently returned from the Peninsular War. It is said that the inn's name was changed to humour them, and came from 'casa de salter', a phrase the soldiers had brought back with them, meaning dancing house. A third suggestion is that the name was put up after a landlord had gone bankrupt by giving credit. The new landlord wished to avoid the same pitfall and made this clear.

Castleton's Oak (Biddenden, Kent) Recalls the story of a local character, the village

Tonbridge, Kent

carpenter. On his seventieth birthday a great oak nearby was destroyed and believing it to be a portent, made his own coffin and contrived to have it always near him. Happily he did not need it for some 30 years.

Cat & Bagpipes (East Harlsey, Yorks) The Scottish Border raiders were known as 'cats' and no doubt some of their number played the bagpipes.

Cat & Cabbage (Rotherham, Lancs) The cap badge of the now disbanded York & Lancaster Regiment represented a tiger and a cabbage rose and it is the badge which now adorns the sign.

Cat & Cracker (Grain, Kent) Whilst the sign shows a cat being startled by a cracker, the name of the inn is derived from a catalytic cracker at the nearby oil refinery.

Cat & Custard Pot (Shipton Moyne, Wilts) This well-known sign is very splendid and recalls R. S. Surtees' famous novel *Handley Cross* published in 1845, with tales of the sporting grocer, John Jorrocks MFH. Sur-

tees, a prolific writer, had a horror of seeing his name in print and avoided it whenever he could.

Cat & Fiddle Usually illustrates on its sign a cat playing a fiddle. There are many theories as to its origin. The most likely is that it is a mispronunciation of Caton le Fidele, a knight who held Calais for the English king. So faithful Caton is commemorated all over the country on numerous signs. The inn of the name on the Cheshire boundary near Buxton is the highest licenced premises in Britain. It stands 1690ft above sea level.

Cat i' th' Window (Halifax, Yorks) Said to be a corruption of Catherine's window, a particular type of circular window to be found in the local parish churches.

Catash (North Cadbury, Som) The name comes from Saxon days when the area was in the Hundred of Catsash and the court was held beneath the ash trees on a site still known as the Three Ashes.

Catherine Wheel A fairly‑popular sign which is believed to have emanated from the badge of the Knights of St Catherine of Sinai, one of the many knightly orders founded to protect pilgrims to the Holy Land. The saint herself was a virgin of royal descent, who publicly confessed the christian faith. By the Emperor Maximinus' decree, she was put to death by torture using a wheel with cutting edges.

Cats (Woodham Walter, Essex) A humorous sign, it shows a number of felines carrying out their ablutions—good lickers, drawing attention to the 'good liquors' obtainable at the inn.

Caxton Gibbet (Nr Caxton, Cambs) The inn is near the site of the old Caxton gibbet, customarily erected at crossroads where their grisly burdens should be a summary lesson to all, particularly highwaymen. Early in the eighteenth century a man committed a murder nearby but escaped to America. Seven years later he returned, talked indiscreetly and was arrested; a birthmark led to

Brinnington, Cheshire

his identification. The record says 'he was hanged alive'. A gibbet still occupies the site. See also *Gibbet*.

C.B. (Langthwaite, Yorks) One of the shortest of inn names. It once served the lead miners from the nearby mines which were the property of Charles Bathurst, lord of the manor. His initials were stamped on every 'pig' of lead that was mined. There is another inn at Arkengarthdale (Yorks) which has his full name *Charles Bathurst*.

Chalk Drawers (Olney Heath, Bucks) The sign shows men loading chalk. The trade was a local industry.

Champion (Well Street, London) Commemorates Sir Gordon Richards who was champion jockey many times over a period of thirty years. In his career he broke the world record with 4970 winners. He was knighted in 1953. There is also a *Champion*

Newark, Nottinghamshire

Jockey named in his honour at Donnington, Salop, close to his birthplace.

Charles XII A racehorse which won the St Leger in 1839. The horse was walked from York to Doncaster for the race, and was eventually sold for 3000 guineas.

Cheese Rollers (Shurdington, Glos) The picturesque sign depicts a local Whit Monday custom over 400 years old. Associated with the traditional rights of local farmers and shepherds to graze their sheep on the common land, a race to secure a cheese rolled from the top of a hill is a pursuit only for the toughest of the local youth.

Chequers There are several suggestions as to the origin of the sign but the fact that a sign resembling a draughtsboard was found in Pompeii lends weight to the theory that the sign was used by innkeepers who also acted as money changers. The chequered board was used to assist in reckoning. This would explain why many of the estimated 300 *Chequers* signs are to be found in seaports. It is also suggested that such a sign proclaimed that chequers could be played over a glass of wine.

Cherry Pickers (Folkestone, Kent) Not fruit pickers but a reminder of the 11th Hussars who bore the nickname by reason of the cherry pink breeches of their uniform. The regiment was at one time stationed at nearby Shornecliffe camp. There are many signs commemorating the old militia and county regiments.

Cheshire Lines (Southport, Merseyside) Recalls a railway branch line which once ran from Cheshire to Southport.

Chieftain (Morecambe, Lancs) Named after a ship which, well known locally, carried a chieftain as its figurehead.

Childe of Hale (Hale, Lancs) The sign, as all good signs should, indicates the story behind the name. It portrays the giant, John Middleton, who was born in the village in 1578 and in his prime stood 9ft 3in tall and was famed as a wrestler. He died at the age of

45 years. The inn today displays an outline of his hand, which measures 8½in across and 17in from wrist to fingertip. He was buried in the local cemetery. See also *Daniel Lambert*.

Chindit (Wolverhampton, Staffs) Named after the famous troops of General Wingate who in the 1939-45 war operated in the Malay jungle behind the Japanese lines. The name comes from the lions of Burmese and Malayan sculpture and architecture, which were adopted as a badge by the troops.

Chopper (Battersea, London) The sign shows a helicopter in flight, 'chopper' being the nickname for the machine.

Church House There are a number of inns of this name, invariably close to the parish church, the reason being that they were once church property. After the Reformation, it was the practice of churchwardens to buy or receive malt to brew beer and many churches had their own brewhouses. The ales were used for the many festivities of the church, including Church Ales, Whitsun Ales and Bid Ales. This last was an excuse to get people together for an entertainment to raise funds as a benefit 'when any honest man decayed in his estate and was set up again by the liberal benevolence and contributions of friends at a feast'. In the west of England, Bid Ales were usually known as Help Ales. Many church inns remain the property of the Church.

Clanger (Houndsditch, London) The reference here is to the bell of the old fire engines, for nearby was the Bishopsgate fire station. The theme of the inn is the great fire of London.

Clayhall (London E3) Takes its name from the Clayhall tavern and tea gardens, which were popular in the last century.

Clickers A sign to be found in Leicester, it was the name given to shoe workers.

Clog & Billycock (Pleasington, Lancs) Formerly the *Bay Horse* the name was changed by popular consent as a tribute to a licensee, Alfred Pomfret, of the 1940s who

Marldon, near Paignton, Devon

Pleasington, Lancashire

was well known on account of his distinctive attire. He always wore clogs and a billycock— a low-crowned hard felt hat. The clogs were a specially made high lace-up boot type, designed by his brother, who was a clogger. For nearly 30 years it was the nickname of the inn—now it is official.

Coach & Eight (Newcastle-upon-Tyne) There are many *Coach & Horses* but this one is unique, for the sign pictures a rowing eight.

Coal Exchange (Fareham, Hants) There was a considerable coal trade in the vicinity which for some strange reason was known locally as 'ickyboo'. See also *Coal House*.

Coal House (Apperly, Glos) The sign shows men carrying coal from a barge to a warehouse. See also *Coal Exchange*.

Cock An ancient sign which comes from Greek mythology. The bird heralds the coming day, symbolising the rising of the sun; such signs are numerous. See also *Fighting Cocks*.

Cock & Pye (Ipswich, Suffolk) This was an old Catholic oath 'By God and the Pie' or 'By God and the Pyx'. Another possible explanation is that it derives from Cock & Magpie.

Cogers (Salisbury Square, London) Takes the name of the oldest debating society in the country and one which, since 1755 when it was founded, has been associated with London's inns. The society has had a variety of homes, the meetings are informal and noisy and the proceedings are unique. The atmosphere is said to be like that which existed in the old London coffee houses.

Commercial In the early part of the century there were hundreds of this name. Now they are rare and the sign at Killay, Glam, shows an old-time traveller or representative.

Commonwealth (Caterham, Surrey) The splendid sign shows the flags of ten countries.

Coney (West Wickham, Kent) The correct name for a rabbit.

Coach & Horses
Sherborne, Dorset

Killay, Glamorgan

Corsair, Birkenhead, Cheshire

Covered Wagon, Moseley, Birmingham

Cook's Ferry (Enfield, Middx) Named after Matthew Cook who ran the ferry which had been a family occupation for generations. Quite an eccentric, his fourteen cats accompanied him on every crossing.

Cornkist (Stirling, Scotland) The sign shows a plough and indicates the centre of an extensive area where the farming of grain is carried out.

Cornubia (Camborne, Cornwall) This is latinised 'Cornwall'. The sign displays the arms of the Duke of Cornwall.

Corsair (Birkenhead, Ches) There is an eye-catching sign of a pirate with raised cutlass.

Cottar (Luton, Beds) A new inn and a new name. A cottar was, up to the nineteenth century, an agricultural worker, immortalised in Robert Burns' *Cotter's Saturday Night*.

Coulter's A name to be found frequently in the border country, where it is a term for a ploughman.

Country Members (Lympne, Kent) The unusual name recalls the County Members, trustees of the Cinque Ports, who administered their own court and dispensed justice. The inn is more than 200 years old and has the distinction of having entertained many pioneer fliers, visitors to the local airfield. In the visitors book are such names as Jean Batten and Captain Bill Lancaster.

Coverdale (Paignton, Devon) Commemorates Miles Coverdale (1488-1568) the remarkable Yorkshireman who first completed a translation of the bible which appeared in 1535. He became Bishop of Exeter in 1551 but was forced to leave the country on the accession of Queen Mary.

Covered Wagon (Moseley, Birmingham) A name that was chosen at random—the theme inside the inn is in keeping with the title. It is unusual in having a carving instead of a conventional inn sign.

Cricketers The popularity of the game ensures a large number of inns so named.

CROSS HANDS

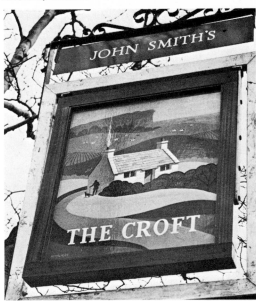

THE CROFT

The counties of Surrey and Yorkshire can probably boast the largest number. Signs are usually very attractive as that at Selby, Yorks, where a two-sided sign shows a young cricketer in a red jacket and a traditional village cricketing scene. See also *Three Willows*.

Crocodile (Danehill, Sussex) The name is not identified with the reptile but is a reminder of the 'tongs' used by smugglers in the eighteenth century to retrieve contraband which had been 'sunk' in tidal water.

Crooked Billet A billet is a small log, from which inn signs were traditionally made.

Crooked Spire (Chesterfield, Derbys) The parish church in the town has a twisted spire, 228ft high. Made of lead-covered wood, it has warped over the centuries and acquired the curious twist.

Crossed Hands A symbol of unity and friendship. Also found as *Cross Hands*.

Crossed Keys Religious in origin, it referred

Cross Keys

Rode, Somerset

sometimes to the keys of St Peter, and often to the insignia of an abbot. The symbol is found on the arms of the Sees of several cathedrals which are dedicated to St Peter. Often found as *Cross Keys*.

Crown There are over a thousand inns so named, obviously as a compliment to the Royal House and resulting from the traditional English affection for the monarchy.

Crown & Cushion Based on royal insignia, the crown is carried on a cushion before the king in the coronation and other ceremonies.

Crown & Mitre Once very popular, it represented the two authorities—Royalty and the Church.

Crown & Stirrup (Lyndhurst, Hants) Relates to the connection between the Crown and the 'stirrup' which was once used by the Verderers Court to measure hunting dogs.

Crown Inn and Old Treaty (Uxbridge, Middx) As the name implies, a treaty was negotiated here in 1645 during the Civil War. Charles I and the Parliamentarians met but were unable to come to an agreement.

Cruel Sea (London NW3) Named after the famous novel written by Nicholas Monsarratt and published in 1951, the story was based on his experiences in the Royal Navy during the 1939-45 war.

Crutched Friar (Nr the Minories, London) In latin *cruciatei* means crossed. The Canon's Regular of the Holy Cross, a minor order of Friars, they wore a cross embroidered on their dress. Founded in Bologna in 1169, the Order first came to England in 1244.

Crystal Palace The building that housed the Great Exhibition of 1851. There is also a sign, *The Glasshouse* at Liverpool. See also *Paxtons Head* and *Sir Joseph Paxton*.

Cuckoo Bush (Gotham, Notts) The village was for centuries proverbial for the folly of its inhabitants. One of the tales was of the men joining hands round a thorn bush to keep a cuckoo inside.

Bass Charrington

The Crown

Frome, Somerset

Cumberland Wrestlers (Carlisle, Cumbria) Commemorates the two famous wrestlers George Steadham and Hexham Clarke. The former was heavyweight champion from 1846 to 1904. The sign shows Steadham on one side and on the reverse the two men engaged in a bout.

Cuttle (Rugby, Warwicks) A canal runs close by—hence the 'cut', and at the rear of the inn was a well. Thus cut-well, shortened to cuttle. The sign shows a cuttlefish.

Cutty Sark (Greenwich, London) There has been an inn on the site for 500 years under various names, but when the famous clipper ship was permanently 'docked' at Greenwich in 1954, the inn took its name. The ship was built for the China tea trade and went into the Australian service, bringing back the wool clip. Fastest of a great line of ships, the average time of her passage from Australia between 1874 and 1890 was 77 days, against 96 days for the rest of the fleet. *Cutty Sark* at Barrow-in-Furness (Lancs) refers not to the ship but to the rough woollen

Mitchells & Butlers

The Cuttle

DALE INN

shirt worn by people in the border country in former days.

Cyprus There are several of the name which probably recall the fact that it was ceded to Britain by the Anglo-Turkish convention in 1878.

Dairy Maid (Aylesbury, Bucks) Takes the name of the pair-horse coach which ran from London to Winslow (Bucks). Achieved some fame when it carried the news of the great victory of Waterloo to Aylesbury, two days after the battle. The news was received in London thirty hours after the victory. The sign of the inn today features the 'Dairy Maid' coach.

Dale (Wallasey, Cheshire) For a great many years this inn, situated in the Merseyside docks area, was a popular meeting place but the time came when it had to be demolished. When it was rebuilt close by John Smiths Tadcaster Brewery and the intention was to rename it 'Carousel' the outcry was immediate and 1000 people petitioned for the retention of the original name. The brewers bowed to public opinion and it remained the *Dale*.

Dandy Roll (London EC4) A dandy roll is a wire roller with which the watermark is put into paper.

Daniel Lambert (Leicester) Another good example of historical fact being kept alive by an inn sign. The subject of this sign was the most corpulent man ever known to have lived in Great Britain. At the age of 23 he tipped the scales at 32 stone. Born in the city, he became keeper of the city's gaol and was made much of when he visited London in 1806. He drank only water and slept less than eight hours a day. When he died in 1809 he weighed $52\frac{3}{4}$ stones and was 5 ft 11 in tall. His coffin required 112 superficial ft of elm. In the museum at Stamford (Lincs) is his waistcoat, which has a girth of 102 in. See also *Childe of Hale*.

Darnley (Nr Holyrood, Edinburgh) Recalls Lord Darnley (1545-67) second husband of

Mary Queen of Scots. Was refused the crown matrimonial, and murdered at Kirk O' Fields, Edinburgh.

David Brewster (Lewisham, London) Named after Sir David Brewster (1781-1868) a Scot who, famous in the study of optics, discovered the kaleidoscope. His portrait appears on the sign.

Daylight (Petts Wood, Kent) The name commemorates a local man, William Willett (1856-1915) who originated daylight saving in this country. A builder by trade, he advocated the innovation by writing a small book 'The Waste of Daylight'. Bills were introduced to Parliament in 1907, 1909 and 1911 but to no avail. It was finally passed in 1916, as a provisional war measure, and has remained ever since. There is another inn of the name in Essex.

Deacon Brodie's (Edinburgh, Scotland) Recalls a notorious local scoundrel of the eighteenth century, William Brodie. He was apprehended when breaking into the general excise department to steal money which brought a number of other crimes to light. He was hanged at the Tolbooth in 1778. There is also a *Deacon's Den* in the city.

Desert Rat (Reigate, Surrey) The nickname of the 7th Armoured Division which served in the Eighth Army throughout the North African campaigns in the 1939-45 war. The divisional sign was a red desert rat on a black background. The 4th Armoured Brigade had a black rat upon a white ground. The name was contemptuously bestowed upon the Brigade by Mussolini, but was adopted with pride by the British units.

Devereux (Westminster, London) Named after Robert Devereux, 2nd Earl of Essex (1566-1601). Gained fame as a soldier and favourite of Queen Elizabeth I until they quarrelled violently. He formed a plot to remove the Queen's ministers and attempted to raise the City of London to revolt. Found guilty of high treason, he was beheaded.

Devil's Elbow (Princetown, Devon) A tricky 'S' bend on the old horse-drawn railway which ran from Plymouth to Princetown is the origin of this unusual name. Built in 1820 to transport goods to the prison and on the return journey peat to Plymouth. The inn originally served as stables and storehouse.

Devil's Stone (Shebbear, Devon) The inn was built in 1678, but has only in recent years had its name changed. It is situated opposite a tremendous stone in front of the church, said to have been dropped by the devil. It is turned over annually lest he be lurking underneath.

Dieu et Mon Droit (Great Stoughton, Herts) Translated is 'God and my right' which was the parole of Richard I at the battle of Gisors (1198). The battle cry was not adopted as the royal motto of England until some 250 years later in the reign of Henry VI.

Dimsdale Arms (Hertford) Thomas Dimsdale (1720-1800) a local man, trained at St Thomas's hospital. Later in private practice he became a pioneer of vaccination

Bass

Deers Leap

Swindon, Wiltshire

against smallpox. He travelled to Russia to vaccinate Catherine the Great and her son at St Petersburg. He received payment of £10,000 together with an annuity of £500 and £2000 expenses. He was created a Baron of the Empire of all the Russias and had the right to add a wing of the Russian eagle to his coat of arms which is featured on the sign.

Dirty Duck (Gloucester) This is unusual. Over the years inns named *Black Swan* were irreverently nicknamed Mucky Duck by the patrons and in some cases the inns have, after a long period, actually been so named. In the same way the *Swan & Sugarloaf* invariably became degraded to the *Duck & Acid Drop*.

Discovery (Cardiff, Glam) Takes the name of the ship in which Captain Robert Falcon Scott (1868-1912) made his voyage to the Antarctic.

Dock Green (Leeds, Yorks) On the site of the former Harehills police station, the inn was named after the long-running television series *Dixon of Dock Green*.

Doctor Johnson (Barkingside, Essex) Named after Dr Samuel Johnson (1709-84). Son of a Lichfield bookseller, he was a prolific writer and in 1755 published his famous dictionary.

Doffcocker (Bolton, Lancs) Takes its name from the village of the name, now a local district. The four-storey building represents the four seasons; has twelve cellars for the months of the year and fifty-two doors for the number of weeks.

Dog (Over, Glos) Legend has it that two men broke into a nearby cottage, attacking and robbing an old lady, and leaving her dead. The culprits were traced to the inn by a dog who followed their trail and from that time the original name, the *Talbot*, was superseded by the *Dog*. The original inn was built in 1754.

Dog & Bacon (Horsham, Sussex) A corruption of Dorking Beacon, which on a clear day can be seen from Horsham.

Dog & Duck Still to be found in many places and usually adjacent to the village pond, for it was associated with a barbaric so-called sport. A duck with pinioned wings was loosed on to the pond and owners then let their dogs free to try and catch the bird. The duck was headed in the direction of the dogs by stones being thrown at it. If the duck survived, drinks were on the masters of the dogs but if it was caught within a set time then the innkeeper supplied the drinks.

Dog in a Doublet (Crowland, Lincs) Two reasonable theories are advanced for the name of this 250-year-old inn. The meaning of doublet in the eighteenth century was a jerkin or loose-fitting waistcoat. When men went hunting or wild fowling, a brightly coloured 'doublet' was placed on the dogs so that they could be clearly seen by the shooting party. The second explanation comes from the old sign which had been preserved, for it shows dogs taking part in a dance, one of them wearing a doublet. In French doublet can mean a form of minuet or dance, thus the dogs are taking part in a 'doublet'. The present sign shows a dog's head peeping out of a poacher's doublet where he had been hidden from the gamekeepers.

Dog Tray (Brighton, Sussex) The name was inspired by a German poem about a dog who was whipped. He retaliated and was able thereafter to sit at board in his master's place. Once very popular, the story formed a sketch on the music halls a hundred years ago.

Donkey & Buskins (Layer-de-la-Haye, Essex) Buskins were leather leggings or gaiters worn by farm workers, and the sign shows a man standing beside a donkey which is wearing them. A farmer called at the inn one night and became the worse for drink. When he left, thinking to protect the donkey's legs from the thorns over the nearby common, he fixed the buskins on the donkey's forefeet. It became a local joke, then a legend, and finally the name of the inn.

Double Gloucester (Gloucester) Named after the cheese of the county, so-called because of the thick double cream it contains which is given by the old Gloucester breed of cows. Many other counties have inns named after their local cheeses, as *Blue Vinny* (Dorset).

Double O Two (Yate, Bristol) A reminder that *Concorde* was built at nearby Filton. The splendid sign shows the plane with two hands extended in a toast—one French, the other British—a mark of the co-operation between the two countries on the project.

Dragon The many differing coloured dragons come from coats of arms. A dragon is featured in the eleventh century Bayeaux tapestry and later appeared in the Tudor coat of arms. See *Red Dragon*.

Driftwood Spars (St Agnes, Cornwall) Over 300 years ago the building served as a marine stores. Then it became an inn, taking its name from the huge spars which serve as beams for the ceiling. They came from shipwrecks and were salvaged from the nearby cove.

Drinker Moth (Harlow New Town, Essex) An example of this most attractive scheme of butterflies and moths as inn signs.

Drum & Monkey (Stamford, Lincs) Many inns over the years have earned and become identified by a nickname created by the 'locals'—this inn is typical. It has had several names but now 'Drum & Monkey' is official. Legend has it that the name arose after a travelling showman halted outside for his monkey to perform tricks on a drum.

Drunken Duck (Hawkshead, Lancs) The tale behind this name is quite amusing. It concerned the innkeeper's wife who discovered several of her ducks lying as if dead in the yard. Thinking they were dead, she started to pluck them whereupon they showed signs of life. It was then discovered that they had found some grain soaked in ale from a leaking barrel. They were drunk, not dead, and the sign shows a merry and convivial duck.

Duchess of Sutherland (Holloway, London) Wife of the 2nd Duke of Sutherland.

WHITBREAD

Double O Two

Yate, Bristol

She was mistress of the robes and a great friend of Queen Victoria.

Duke of Clarence Takes the name of the eldest son of Edward VII. He was betrothed to Princess Mary of Teck, but died when he was twenty-eight years of age before the marriage.

Duke of Cumberland Refers to the second son of George II who had a distinguished military career. His brutality in crushing the 1745 Jacobite rebellion under the Young Pretender at Culloden in 1746 earned him the nickname of 'Butcher' Cumberland. Inns named *Duke William* also refer to him.

Duke of Marlborough After John Churchill (1650-1722) the English general who was the son of Sir Winston Churchill, an impoverished Royalist. After quelling the Monmouth rebellion he was rewarded with a barony. Had supreme command of British forces in the war of the Spanish succession and was loaded with favours by Queen Anne. Blen-

Bass Charrington

PLAN OF BATTLE
MOVEMENT ORDER
10,000 MEN

*...der in Chief.
York.*

Duke of York

Yeovil, Somerset

heim Palace was built and presented to him by the nation.

Duke of Wellington There are probably hundreds of inns which take their name from Arthur Wellesley (1769-1852) created Duke of Wellington in 1814. His brilliant generalship reached its peak in the Peninsular War and ended with the final victory over Napoleon in 1815. There are many variations of the name — *Hero of Waterloo, Iron Duke*, and even the *Dook* at Falmouth (Cornwall) where he is pictured on the sign.

Duke of York There are many inns named after the various Dukes who enjoyed their periods of popularity only to have their portraits on signs superseded by a newcomer. The best known Duke of York was HRH Frederick, the Field Marshal, who marched the troops up the hill and marched them down again. Although an unsuccessful commander, he devoted himself with great courage and vigour to reforms. He is commemorated by the Duke of York column in London. The badge of the Dukes of York has been made up of the sun and rose, and has been used by successive Dukes including George VI, the father of our present Queen.

Dumb Flea (Meldreth, Cambs) Not an attempt at humour but apparently mispronunciation. It was originally the *Dumfries*.

Dun Cow This was the ferocious beast supposed to have been slain by Guy of Warwick. At Warwick Castle there is still a tusk on show, said to have come from the animal. The legend is that the cow gave an inexhaustible milk supply, but it became ferocious as man's greed increased. The beast went berserk, broke loose and had to be killed. Inns of the name have frequently used couplets on their signs:

> Walk in gentlemen, I trust you'll find
> The Dun Cow's milk is to your mind.

Dusty Miller Frequently found in Lancashire and Yorkshire, it is usually situated close to local mills where corn was ground. Often a windmill appears on the sign.

Eagle & Child This is the crest of the Earl of Derby, which dates from Sir John Stanley in the fourteenth century. Legend tells of the finding and adoption of a child in an eagle's nest, and the subsequent use of the incident for the crest.

Earl Canning Commemorates Charles John Canning (1812-62). A politician, he became governor-general of India.

Earl Grey There are several commemorating Charles Grey (1764-1845) who was a brilliant politician and Prime Minister. He carried through the act abolishing the slave trade in Africa and the colonies. He was Prime Minister in 1830 and all his successors in this office until 1895 have their place on inn signs. Since that date only three have been so honoured.

Earl Haig More than one inn carries the name of Douglas Haig (1861-1928) the British field marshal who took the first corps of the BEF to France in 1914. He became Commander-in-Chief in 1915.

Mural in *Empire Bar*, Bath, Somerset

Stratford-upon-Avon, Warwickshire

Early Bird (Nottingham) Modern sign with a satellite on the one side and a bird with a worm on the other.

East India College Arms (Hertford Heath, Herts) Formerly the *Jolly Pindar*, the inn was rebuilt in 1806 by the East India Company.

Eclipse (Tunbridge Wells, Kent) Takes the name of one of the famous coaches, the route of which was through the town.

Eliza Doolittle (Euston Road, London) Named after the character in George Bernard Shaw's successful play *Pygmalion*. It was produced as a film in 1935, again in 1964, and as a musical play titled *My Fair Lady* in 1956.

Empress of Russia (Finsbury, London) Refers to Catherine the Great who, born a Lithuanian peasant, ruled Russia despotically for 43 years.

Encore (Stratford-on-Avon, Warwicks) An effective and fitting sign showing Shakespearean actors 'taking their bow'.

Ensign Ewart (Edinburgh) Remembers an ensign of the Scots Greys who captured a Napoleonic standard at the battle of Waterloo.

Escape (Mabledon Place, London) With barbed wire in close-up, and a prison camp in the background, this is a most effective sign. A tribute to the many hundreds of men from the three services who made their escape from prisoner-of-war camps in the 1939-45 war.

Essex Skipper (Harlow New Town, Essex) One of a series at Harlow named after butterflies and moths.

Ethelbert (Herne Bay, Kent) One of a large number of kings and queens who lend their names to inns. This is the early Saxon king who reigned AD 860-66.

Exmouth Named after Sir Edward Pellew (1757-1833). As commander-in-chief East Indies he destroyed a Dutch fleet. In 1816

Lambeth Walk, London

he bombarded Algiers and rooted out the pirates, for which service he was made Viscount.

Falcon Falconry was a royal sport for hundreds of years and a number of such signs spring from this. A falcon appeared on the crest of Queen Elizabeth and was also a Yorkist sign. The Charing Cross area of London was for centuries the Royal mews where falcons were kept.

Falcon Bearer (Knutsford, Ches) This title is given to the leader of the annual Knutsford carnival.

Farrar's (Greenfield, Yorks) The inn was once the manor house of the Farrar family. It dates back to 1685 and it was then the custom for a flag to be hoisted outside when the tithes were due from the peasants of the district. The family gave them food and drink. The sign depicts the tradition, showing a man before a bench paying his tithe.

Fazakerley (Chorley, Lancs) Named after Nicholas Fazakerley (d 1767) lawyer and politician, recorder and MP for Preston.

Feathers See *Fleur-de-Lys*.

Fellmonger Several in the north country where the trade of fellmongering—dealing in skins—is common.

Fencibles Recalls the regiments of horse and foot militia raised for home service in 1759, 1778 and 1794 totalling a force of 15,000.

Mitchells & Butlers

Flash Harry

West Bromwich, Staffordshire

They were disbanded in 1802. The word is short for defensible.

Fifteen Balls (Penryn, Cornwall) Fifteen roundles arranged in triangular form appear in the Cornish coat of arms. There is also a *Cornish Arms* at Bodmin (Cornwall) which has fifteen half balls in bas relief on the sign.

Fighting Cocks For centuries after the Romans introduced cock fighting into these islands, it had a tremendous popularity. A cockpit was added to Whitehall palace in the reign of Henry VIII as a 'royal diversion'. The sport was prohibited by Cromwell in 1653 but not finally abolished until 1840. Until then many inns had their cockpits, where specially bred birds equipped with cruel steel spurs fought to the death. Even now from time to time there are prosecutions for such gaming. Other variations of the name are *Gamecock, Top Bird, Cock* etc.

First & Last Very frequently found. Refers to the first inn approaching the town and the last leaving it.

Fish Popular probably because they are associated with liquids. The *Three Fishes*, now rare, was a firm favourite in the middle ages, the 'three' representing the Trinity.

Flash Harry (West Bromwich, Staffs) Was originally intended to be named after the man who 'flashed' the furnaces in the area in the early morning. By a series of misunderstandings the sign and murals inside (which still remain) feature the late Sir Malcolm Sargent who received this affectionate nickname from the public.

Fleece A popular sign particularly where sheep and the wool trade flourished. For at least three centuries England's economy rested on wool, which not only provided an easy source of taxation, but financed the wars of several monarchs from the twelfth to the fifteenth centuries. Richard I raised the money for his crusade from wool, and when he was captured and held to ransom, money from wool also provided the means of his release. In the late thirteenth century half the value of the whole country was in wool and in the fourteenth century the annual export value was 7 million pounds. Monks from the great abbeys were prolific sheep breeders, and in the limestone Cotswold area where the grazing was considered the best, enormous wealth was derived, to which the great 'wool' churches still testify. In the Cotswolds there are a great number of inns such as *Fleece, Golden Fleece, Ram* etc. A reminder of the wealth which emanated from wool is the woolsack in the House of Lords, still the official seat of the Lord Chancellor; the name 'woolsack' is often applied to the office. See also *Woolpack*.

Flemish Weaver (Salford, Lancs) The inn is sited in another area where the original Flemish weavers settled when they left the continent during the religious troubles of the sixteenth century. See also *Bay & Say*.

Fletchers Originally a fletcher was a manufacturer of bows and arrows.

Fleur-de-Lys Associated in this country with the badge of the Prince of Wales, which was first adopted by the Black Prince, son of Edward III. The name, meaning lily

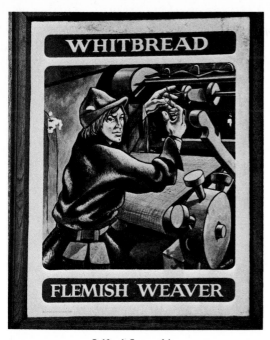

WHITBREAD

FLEMISH WEAVER

Salford, Lancashire

Bass

Foresters Arms

Bath, Somerset

flower, was borne as a charge on the old French coat of arms. Variations include *Feathers*, *Prince of Wales Feathers*, *Plume of Feathers*, etc.

Flint Knappers (Brandon, Suffolk) Obviously designed to attract the men who carried out the job of cracking flints. 'Knappers' comes from the Dutch *knappen*— to crack.

Flying Bull (Rake, Hants) The London to Portsmouth coach route was served by two vehicles, known respectively as the 'Fly' and the 'Bull' and from these the inn takes its name. The place is unique in being built astride the Hampshire/Sussex border, and rates are paid to both county authorities.

Flying Dutchman (Summerbridge, Yorks) The sign, copied from an old print, depicts the famous race between Flying Dutchman and Voltigeur, which took place in 1851.

Flying Monk A unique sign at Malmesbury (Wilts) which recalls the story written by an eleventh-century historian William of Malmsbury about a monk named Elmer who tried to fly. Far ahead of his time, he fastened wings to his hands and feet and leapt from the top of the abbey tower. Naturally he crashed to the ground, escaping lightly with a broken leg, though he was lame thereafter. He reasoned that all might have been well had he provided himself with a tail.

Flying Shuttle (Farnworth, Lancs) A reference to the cotton spinning machinery.

Fort St George in England (Midsummer Common, Cambs) The inn has enjoyed the name since 1520, due to its island position and the similarity to Fort St George, Madras. The sign shows ships approaching an old fort.

Fortune of War (Woolwich, London SE18). The ship of the name is pictured on the sign. It was the most famous of the eighteenth-century privateers, merchant vessels specially armed and manned to attack enemy merchant shipping.

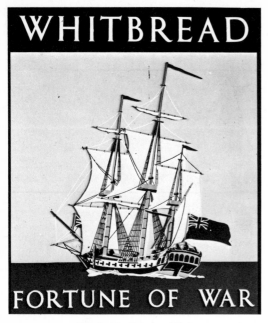

Woolwich, London SE18

Kentisbeare, Devon

Fountain Was a very popular sign in medieval times, possibly on account of the martyrdom of St Paul. When his head was struck off, it rebounded three times and a fountain gushed up at each spot where it touched the ground. The sign is also to be found adjoining the old Roman roads and possibly originally indicated a spring or fountain.

Four Alls An interesting sign which carries four portraits. There are variations but usually they constitute the king who rules over all, parson who prays for all, soldier who fights for all, John Bull who pays for all. An example of ignorance in repainting a sign was the *Four Awls*. There are sometimes *Five Alls* and *Six Alls* which normally include the devil (I take all).

Four Lords (Par, Cornwall) The attractive sign portrays four fashionably-dressed sixteenth-century gallants. They were the lords who jointly owned the local manor.

Foy Boat (Ramsgate, Kent) Carries as its sign a picture of the small specialised craft which plied from Ramsgate, Margate, Broadstairs and Deal to serve vessels lying in the Downs awaiting favourable winds. The trade was a rich one and some skippers of foy boats made as much as £50,000 a year.

Free Trade Recalls that for years this was a hotly contested political theory. Great Britain abandoned the system in 1932.

French Revolution (Putney, London) As most Englishmen were appalled at the happenings in France in the eighteenth century, it is difficult to understand the reason for such a name. The Revolution is usually dated from the storming of the Bastille in 1789. The monarchy was not overthrown until 1792 and France was declared a Republic the same year.

Friar Bacon (Marston, Oxon) After Roger Bacon (1214-92). Born in Somerset, he studied at Oxford and entered a Franciscan Order. A brilliant scientist, he invented the magnifying glass.

THE FOXHOUND

CHARRINGTON

Fivehead, Somerset

Frightened Horse Originally the *Freighted Horse*, a packman's animal. Through ignorance it was incorrectly spelt when the sign was repainted. The error has been deliberately perpetuated in one or two places. See *Horse & Crook* and *Packhorse*.

Furnham (Chard, Somerset) A canal horse used for towing barges on the local canal is featured on the sign. It recalls the 1850s when the Chard Canal, 13½ miles long, was opened for small tub boats. The canal was commenced in 1834, completed in 1842, and closed in 1867.

Garden Tiger (Harlow New Town, Essex) Has a moth on one side of the sign and a fierce-looking tom cat on the other.

Garibaldi (Worcester) Named in honour of Guiseppe Garibaldi (1807-82) the Italian liberator. He visited England and was received with wild enthusiasm but was asked to leave by the government.

Garrick The famous eighteenth-century actor David Garrick (1717-79) has several signs in his honour. Considered the most versatile actor in history of the British stage.

Gate Normally to be found where once stood a toll gate on a thoroughfare. There are many variations. *The Gate Hangs Well* at Syston (Leics) is a five-barred gate carrying the legend:

> This gate hangs well and hinders none,
> Refresh and pay, and travel on.

Gay Gordon After George, 5th Duke of Gordon (1770-1836) who raised the regiment of Gordon Highlanders in 1795 and commanded it in Corsica, Spain, Ireland and Holland. A variety of signs in Scotland refer to him—*Heiland Laddie*, *Cock o' the North*, *Huntly Arms*.

General Allenby (Nr Wimborne, Dorset) Named after a successful 1914-18 war general, Viscount Allenby (1861-1936). Famous for his firm measures in Egypt and Palestine.

General Elliott (1717-90) Distinguished soldier who won fame at Gibraltar which he defended against the Spaniards in 1779-83. Was created first Baron Heathfield.

General Grant (Poplar, London) Commemorates Ulysses Grant (1822-85), famous general of the northern states in the American Civil War. Became President of the United States 1868 and 1872. A proposal for a third term was not approved.

General Havelock Named after Sir Henry Havelock (1795-1857) distinguished soldier of the Indian Mutiny.

General Rawdon (Luddenden Foot, Yorks) Refers to General Sir George Rawdon (1604-84) who fought under General Monck in the Irish rebellion and played an active part in the restoration of the monarchy.

General Wade (Leeds, Yorks) As commander-in-chief Scotland in 1724, he pacified and disarmed the Highlands after the Jacobite Rebellion, 1715. He constructed a system of metalled military roads including 40 bridges which bear his name.

General Wolfe (Westerham, Kent) The name does honour to James Wolfe, born at the local vicarage in 1727. A brilliant military career was ended when he was killed on the Plains of Abraham, Canada, fighting the French in 1759.

Gentil Knyght (Canterbury, Kent) One of the many inns named from the period of the religious fervour of the Crusades. Another is the *White Knight*, Crawley (Sussex).

George Though in later times the name often stood for one of the Hanoverian kings, in medieval times it was shortened from St George and the dragon, with a sign showing the knight on horseback transfixing a dragon. In 1344, on St George's Day, the Order of St George was created by Edward III and St George was thereafter regarded as the patron saint of England. There are some excellent signs in this category. Some signs refer to the Hanoverian kings by carrying a likeness of one of the four Georges and there is one of George V at Ilford (Essex). See *George & Dragon*.

George & Dragon Refers to the patron saint of England since the institution of the Order of the Garter in the mid fourteenth century. The legend of St George and the dragon is an allegorical expression of the victory of the Christian hero over evil. The war cry of the English soldiers at the French wars was 'St George for England'. See *George*.

George & Pilgrims (Glastonbury, Som) An inn founded by a religious community to accommodate the more wealthy pilgrims who journeyed to Glastonbury. At the Dissolution the abbey was destroyed and the hostel became a secular inn.

George in a Tree (Nr Coventry, Warwicks) Was formerly the *Royal Oak*, a popular sign celebrating the escape of Charles II by hiding in a tree. The innkeeper who lacked historical knowledge and wishing to be up-to-date substituted George III when his sign was repainted. See also *Royal Oak*.

Gibbet There is sometimes an inn of this macabre name where a gibbet once existed.

WHITBREAD

GILBERT & SULLIVAN

The Strand, London

The bodies of executed persons were hung in chains from its projecting arm.

Gilbert & Sullivan (Strand, London) Commemorates the famous combination of Sir William S. Gilbert (1839-1911) and Sir Arthur Sullivan (1842-1900) who collaborated to produce charming light opera for the D'Oyly Carte Opera Company. Gilbert was responsible for the lyrics and Sullivan for the music. Their first joint work was in 1871 and for nearly 30 years their output was prolific. D'Oyly Carte built the Savoy theatre especially for their operas. It seems a little unfair that only Gilbert's portrait appears on the sign.

Giles (Islington, London) A rarity insofar as it is a new inn opened and named after a man in his own time. It refers to Carl Ronald Giles, born in Islington, who achieved fame as a cartoonist of the *Daily Express* newspaper. Trained as an animated cartoonist, he produced and animated documentary films for the Government in World War II. He was also a war correspondent-cartoonist.

Gipsy Moth IV (Plymouth, Devon) The name of Sir Francis Chichester's yacht in which he accomplished the lone voyage round the world. See *Lone Yachtsman*.

Globe In previous centuries always a popular name particularly in places where the inn could rely on cosmopolitan patronage. The sign today is usually a terrestrial globe. An exceptionally good one, showing Sir Francis Drake and his *Golden Hind* in the background is at Sampford Peverell (Som).

Gloster Flying Machine Attractive sign at Brockworth (Glos). Refers to the famous eighteenth-century stage coach which ran from London to Gloucester.

Glovers Needle (Worcester) The spire of St Andrew's church is known locally by the name. The city was once closely associated with the glove trade.

Gnu (Stedham, Sussex) More than 60 varieties of the animal world appear on signs. The gnu is one of the more unusual. It is a wildebeest or antelope—the name came from the Kaffir *nqu*.

Goat & Compasses Believed to be a corruption of 'God Encompasses Us', originally a Puritan motto during the Commonwealth. Whether its present form was accident or design is not known.

Goat in Boots (Fulham, London) An old sign certainly known in 1663. The original sign at Fulham was painted by the artist George Morland. The goat was always popular in signs but there is no apparent reason why the animal was given boots.

Golden Arrow (Folkestone, Kent) Named after the famous London to Dover rail service for Paris which ran for 43 years until 1973. The sign shows the train.

Golden Fleece A popular sign in sheep country. The signs often show a sheep with a band around its middle. This was the badge of the Knightly Order of the Golden Fleece, founded by the Duke of Burgundy in 1430. See also *Fleece, Ram, Woolpack*.

Golden Hind Several in the Westcountry

GLOBE

Sampford Peverell, Devon

are named after the ship in which the Devon sailor Sir Francis Drake (1540-96) circumnavigated the world (1580). He was knighted by Queen Elizabeth on his ship at Deptford. See also *Sir Francis Drake*.

Golden Knight (Huntingdon) The sobriquet of Sir Henry Cromwell, an ambitious and wealthy man, who in the sixteenth century earned the nickname 'Golden Knight' due to his lavish expenditure on his family home Hinchingbrooke House, formerly a monastery. The house is now a grammar school.

Golden Swift (Harlow New Town, Essex) Rich colours portray the moth of the name.

Goldfinger (Highworth, Wilts) Named after one of the characters created by Ian Fleming (1908-64), who in his short fifty-six years was author, journalist, banker, stockbroker, foreign manager of the *Sunday Times* and served with British Intelligence in World War II.

Good Intent (Fareham, Hants) The sign

Bass

![image: illustration of a sailing cutter with a framed badge reading "GOOD INTENT 8 GUN NAVAL CUTTER 1787"]

Good Intent

Fareham, Hampshire

WHITBREAD

GREAT ENGINEER

Bristol

shows an inshore cutter of the type designed for coastal defence around 1800.

Grand Trunk (Birkenhead, Ches) Commemorates the building of the Leeds & Liverpool Canal, opened in 1816. It took 46 years to complete the 127 miles and cost nearly $1\frac{1}{4}$ million pounds.

Grave Maurice (Whitechapel Road, London) This refers to Count Maurice of Nassau (1567-1625) son of William the Silent and afterwards Prince of Orange. As a soldier he confounded all the power of Spain, compelling the acceptance of the United Provinces as a free republic.

Great Engineer (Bristol) Honours Isambard Brunel, the engineering genius. See also *Isambard Brunel*.

Great Harry (Hemel Hempstead, Herts) The first double-decked warship in the English navy was built in 1512 and named 'Henry Grace a Dieu' after Henry VIII. The three-masted vessel pictured on the sign was about 1500 tons, had 72 guns and carried a crew of 700.

Great White Horse (Ipswich, Suffolk) This was described vividly by Charles Dickens who stayed there while working as a reporter on the *Ipswich Chronicle*. The scenes which he described in *Pickwick Papers* may be recalled in the virtually unaltered surroundings today including the four-poster bed; the inn was well known as far back as 1518.

Green Man A very popular sign in most parts of England. He was a prominent figure in pagan May Day dancing, when a youth moved about the revels encased in a wicker framework covered with leaves and boughs. It was part of the chimney sweep revels, an English custom now dead. The Green Man is also depicted on signs as a forester, a verderer, or even Robin Hood. See *Jack-in-the-Green*.

Green Star This is the symbol of the Esperanto society which promotes an artificial language intended to be universal.

Greycoat Boy (Greenwich, London) Recalls the famous school founded in London, 1698. Once co-educational, it is now restricted to girls.

Greyfriars Bobby (Edinburgh) Takes the name of a shaggy little Skye terrier who was a legend in his own time. Every day the dog visited his master's grave throughout the 14 years that he out-lived him, leaving only for food. When he died Baroness Burdett-Coutts had a bronze effigy made which is additional to the sign outside the inn where the little dog went daily for his meals. An epic of mute but eloquent faithfulness.

Greyhound A sign which dates from the Tudor kings, it appeared on the coats of arms of both Henry VII and VIII. Until late in the eighteenth century a silver greyhound was worn on the sleeve of the kings' messengers. Some later signs refer to the sport of coursing.

Guinea Pig (East Grinstead, Sussex) A reminder of the hospital close by which specialised in plastic surgery during the 1939-45 war period. The inn is named after the Guinea Pig Club which comprised some 600 men of fourteen nationalities. They were in the main pilots and aircrew of the allied nations, who were treated at the hospital where the great surgeon Sir Archibald McIndoe was the guiding spirit.

Gunners (Nr Liverpool) Named after the local speedway team, the sign is unique in depicting a speedway rider.

Gurkha (Iver, Bucks) A tribute to the fine fighting men from Nepal who have served Britain well. The first regiment was raised in 1815 and eventually ten regiments were formed, six of which have now been transferred to the Indian Army.

Hadrian's Wall (Hexham, Northumb) History is perpetuated by the sign which draws attention to the great Roman rampart which runs for $73\frac{1}{2}$ miles between Wallsend-on-Tyne and Bowness on the Solway Firth. Built by the Emperor Hadrian nearly 2000 years ago, it was designed to keep back the

WHITBREAD

HALF CROWN

Hereford

north British tribes. Some 20ft high and 8ft thick, there were strong towers at each mile of its length.

Half Butt Refers to the large cask used for wine or beer. A butt contains 126 gallons of wine or 108 gallons of beer. See *Three Tuns*.

Half Crown (Hereford) Although Britain's Chambers of Commerce approved a decimal coinage scheme in 1917, it was not brought into being until 1971. Half crowns ceased to be legal tender in December 1969.

Halfway House Usually to be found on the old main roads and having the obvious meaning—between two towns.

Hansom Cab Named after the two-wheeled hackney carriage which was in popular use in cities in the nineteenth century. Its inventor was Joseph Hansom, an English architect.

Hare & Hounds Always a popular sign with many variations of design. The John Smiths

Bar murals from *The Hare & Hounds*, Corsham, Wiltshire

Tadcaster Brewery sign at Birkenhead is an amusing one showing the hare overlooking two hounds arrayed as huntsmen.

Hark to Bounty There are a number of variations—*Hark to Mopsey*, etc. In hunting country a hound whose baying was distinctive and could thus easily be distinguished often became a favourite to be given the accolade of an inn sign. Such names are popular in the north country.

Harnser (Catfield, Norfolk) In Norfolk dialect the word means a heron.

Harrier (Hamble, Hants) The Harrier in this case is the aircraft which was developed by a local aircraft company.

Havelock Commemorates General Sir Henry Havelock (1795-1857). A distinguished soldier who fought through the Afghanistan campaign and the Indian mutiny.

Dalston, London

He relieved Cawnpore and saw the horrors of the massacre, and he held Lucknow until the siege was relieved.

Hawk & Buckle The most acceptable explanation is that the word buckle is a corruption of the French *boucle* meaning swivel or staple. When a hawk is not flying free it is secured to a block by a long leash which terminates in a swivel. Another expression is *en boucle* meaning imprisoned.

Hawkins Usually honours the Elizabethan sea-dog Sir John (1532-95) who undertook various voyages. Commander of the rear squadron against the Spanish Armada.

Heart & Club (Harlow New Town, Essex) The moth of the name appears on the sign.

Help me Through this World Derived from the seventeenth-century punishment for drunkards—the drunkard's cloak—a tub with holes for the arms of the culprit to pass through when he was put inside for his misdemeanours.

Henry Holland (London W1) The famous architect (1746-1806) who designed Battersea Bridge, Brighton Pavilion and enlarged Carlton House. He also planned Sloane Street.

Henry Jenkins (Kirkby Malzeard, Yorks) Carries the name of the man who claimed to have been born in 1501 and lived until 1667. Certainly he had a long life span but there is no proof that he lived for 166 years. See also *Old Parr's Head.*

Hermit (Burley-in-Wharfedale, Yorks) Recalls the eccentric character known as 'Old Job', who lived in the area a hundred years ago. The illegitimate son of a wealthy landowner, at the age of 60 he married an 80-year-old widow and on her death lived in a hovel measuring only 3 ft by 5 ft. Crowds used to go to the woods in the hope of catching a glimpse of him. He died in 1857, aged 77. The inn, formerly the *Woolpack*, was renamed so that he should be remembered.

Hero Several of this name have a likeness to Lord Nelson on their signs. At Burnham Overy, Staithe, Norfolk, there had been an inn of the name for many years and it was suggested by the brewers that Nelson should be replaced on the sign by Wing Commander Guy Gibson, VC who led the Dambusters in the 1939-45 war. There was a local outcry against the change and Admiral Nelson still graces the signboard.

Hero of Aliwal (Whittlesey, Northants) Commemorates Sir Harry Smith (1787-1860) a local man who became a brilliant soldier, serving through the Peninsular War and the Sikh campaign. Distinguished himself in leading a charge at the Battle of Aliwal in 1846. Towns named after him in South Africa where he is similarly honoured include Harrismith and Ladysmith (his wife).

Hero of Switzerland (Brixton, London) Named after William Tell, legendary hero of his native district in Switzerland. He refused to comply with the tyrannical rule of Austria and was condemned to shoot an apple from his son's head. He succeeded and afterwards slew the Austrian tyrant. It is doubtful whether Tell ever really existed.

H.H. (Cheriton, Hants) The letters represent the monogram of the Hampshire Hunt which was in fact the original name of the inn.

Higgler (Nottingham) The name given to the men who carried provisions about for sale.

Hobby Horse (Minehead, Som) The sign shows a traditional hobby horse comprised of a light frame of wickerwork appropriately draped, in which someone gambolled in the ancient morris dances held at May Day festivals.

Hobson's Choice (Warwick) British expression for no choice at all, which stems from Thomas Hobson, a Cambridge carrier, who lived in the seventeenth century. He would only allow the horses he had for hire to be used in strict rotation—thus it was 'Hobson's choice'.

Hole in the Wall Theories regarding its

HOLMAN CLAVELL

Culmhead, Somerset

HONITON INN
Traditional Honiton Lace

WHITBREAD

Exeter, Devon

origin are numerous. Verses 7-10, chapter VIII of the book of Ezekiel '. . . and when I looked in, behold a hole in the wall', appear to be relevant, though the subsequent verses would hardly seem to confirm it. Another supposition is that it referred to the hole in the wall of a debtors prison, through which food was passed. Its most likely origin is that it came from inns snugly sited in a passage in or near the town walls. It was at the *Hole in the Wall*, Chandos Street, London, that Claude Duval, the highwayman, was captured when drunk and hanged at Tyburn 1670.

Holford (Knockdown, Glos) Honours Robert Stayner Holford who planned and founded the arboretum at Westonbirt. He was squire of the village and started his collection of trees in 1829. The sign shows his coat of arms superimposed on a tree.

Holman Clavell (Culmhead, Som) A clavell is a local word for a beam over a fireplace; holman is derived from holly. There is a very heavy holly beam across the fireplace in the bar and this is featured on the sign.

Honest Lawyer (King's Lynn, Norfolk) Humorous sign which shows a lawyer holding his head in his hand.

Honiton A splendid sign in Exeter shows some Honiton lace for which the town of Honiton in Devon is famous.

Hooden Horse (Wickhambreaux, Kent) A figure associated with morris dancing. See also *Morris Dancer*.

Hopcroft's Holt (Steeple Ashton, Oxon) The original inn was a haunt of Claude Duval, the highwayman who was apprehended in 1670 and hanged when only 27 years old. The sign carries a likeness of Duval.

Hop Pole Set up as a sign in honour of hops, without which beer could not be made, in the same way as the vine was used for wine shops. A famous *Hop Pole* is at Tewkesbury (Glos) which was mentioned by Charles Dickens in his writings.

Ivybridge, Devon

Awliscombe, Devon

Horns (Nursling, Hants) Horns were always sounded to announce the approach of heavy drays, for horses were changed at the inn after the pull up Horns Hill. The public bar at the inn once served as the mortuary and the nearby hamlet is named Toot Hill. The sign is by Stanley Chew.

Horse & Chains (Bushey, Herts) The name is a reminder of the days of horse transport when additional horses, fitted with spiked shoes, were stationed at the bottom of local Clay Hill to assist heavily-laden waggons to the top.

Horse & Crook Crooks were the wooden panniers hinged and equipped with a pin, fitted to hang down the sides of pack horses. They were much used in the Westcountry. See *Packhorse, Frightened Horse*.

Hour Glass The name recalls the method of recording the passing hours in earlier days. Most churches in the seventeenth century had them attached to the pulpit so that the preacher could time his sermon.

Hoy There are several of the name near the river Thames, for a hoy was a coasting ketch or yawl, formerly a sloop.

Hufflers The men who ferried goods from ships chandlers to the ships at anchor off-shore. There are a wide variety of trade or craft signs obviously set up in the first place to attract the business of men of a particular calling. They make a formidable list from bakers to well-diggers and wheelwrights.

Humming Bird (Harlow New Town, Essex) Not the bird but the moth of the name appears on the sign.

Independent (London N1) Named in honour of Louis Kossuth (1802-94) leader of the Hungarian revolution in 1848. His extra-ordinary energy in prosecuting a war made him a hero. He was received with enthusiasm in England and the United States. Before he died he wrote a *History of Hungary*. See also *Louis Kossuth*.

Indian Queen (Boston, Lincs) Refers to Pocahontas (1595-1617) an American Indian princess. She twice saved the life of Captain John Smith who assisted in colonising Virginia. He was born at Willoughby (Lincs). She took the Christian religion, married an Englishman and returned to this country with him in 1616. Several Virginian families claim descent from her.

Inkerman Remembers the desperately fought infantry action during the Crimean War, 1854. The battle was indecisive.

Intrepid Fox (London) There are hundreds of signs referring to the animal, but this one recalls Charles James Fox (1749-1806) third son of the 1st Lord Holland. A politician, he made his mark as an opponent of the coercive measures of the government during the American War of Independence.

Isambard Brunel (Bristol) Commemorates the great engineer, Isambard Kingdom Brunel (1806-59) who was closely associated with the city. He designed the Temple Meads railway station and his steamship, the *Great Britain,* built in 1839 is now in the city basin.

Gloucester

There is a *Brunel* at Saltash, by the bridge he designed. See also *Atmospheric Railway* and *Great Engineer*.

Jack in the Green He figured prominently in the pagan May Day revels. See also *Green Man*.

Jack o' Lantern (South Ockendon, Essex) Is another name for Will o' the Wisp, the flame-like phosphorescence which flits over marshy ground (due to spontaneous com-bustion of gas from decaying vegetable matter) eluding those who attempt to catch it.

Jack Russell (Swimbridge, Devon) Named after the famous nineteenth-century hunting parson, who bred the original Jack Russell terriers.

Jacob's Ladder Another medieval religious sign at one time very numerous. Refers to the ladder seen by Jacob in a vision—Genesis Ch 28; v 12.

Jacob's Post (Ditchling Common, Sussex)

There has been an inn on the site for more than 200 years but the name was changed soon after Jacob Harris, a highwayman, was hanged on the nearby gibbet. He murdered three people at the inn after robbing them, was apprehended and executed. Because he was the last man to be left in chains on the gibbet, the inn has been known ever since as *Jacob's Post*. Still standing, it bears the date 1734.

Jacob's Well Once a popular religious sign.

Jenny Lind Named after the famous Swedish singer acclaimed as the 'Swedish nightingale'. Born in humble circumstances in Stockholm in 1820, she performed on the stage at an early age. From 1849 she sang only at concerts using her fees in founding and endowing musical scholarships in England and Sweden. She married Otto Goldschmidt, her pianist, in 1852. She died at Malvern (Worcs) in 1887.

Jet & Whittle (Gloucester) The first flights of the Gloster jet-propelled aeroplane with an engine designed by Sir Frank Whittle, took place from Gloster Aircraft Works in 1941. The sign shows the aircraft sign-writing the name 'Whittle'.

John Baird (London N10) Named after John Logie Baird (1888-1946) who pioneered television. He studied electrical engineering in Glasgow and began television research in 1922. His first true demonstration was in January 1926, and the first transatlantic transmission in colour came two years later. His system was used by the BBC from 1929 until 1937.

John Bunyan (Coleman Green, Herts) The famous author (1628-88) whose *Pilgrim's Progress* was published in 1678. This work sold 100,000 copies in his lifetime and became a classic. The chimney stack of his former cottage is pictured on the sign.

John Burns The politician (1859-1943) who was president of the Board of Trade in 1914 but resigned on the outbreak of war. He was the first 'working man' to achieve Cabinet rank in parliament.

Salford, Lancashire

John Evelyn (Deptford, Wilts) Named after the English diarist and author (1620-1706).

John of Gaunt A great many of the *Red Lion* inns, and there are hundreds in the country, originate from the badge of John of Gaunt (1340-99) but there are several signs showing the man himself who was the most influential figure in the realm.

John Peel Found in several places in the Lake District, this recalls John Peel (1776-1854) who for 55 years maintained a style and pace as a huntsman remarkable even among the Lake District enthusiasts. His worldwide reputation is largely due to the song written about him 'D'ye ken John Peel'.

John Snow (Soho, London) John Snow (1813-58) discovered that cholera was communicated by contaminated water. He also introduced the scientific use of ether into English surgical practice and administered chloroform to Queen Victoria at the birth of Prince Leopold, 1853.

Jubilee A great many inns were so named to

Pelynt, Cornwall

Maesteg, Glamorgan

celebrate the jubilee of Queen Victoria who ascended the throne in 1837, celebrated her 50 years' reign in 1887 and her diamond jubilee 10 years later. She died in 1901 aged 81 years.

Judge's Keep (Glenluce, Cumbria) The name has no definite historical significance. In earlier days the Stair family were involved in administering justice and had a residence at Carlisle. It might have some connection.

Jugg's (Kingston, Sussex) These were the men who regularly carried fish from Brighton to Lewes.

Karozzin (Preston, Lancs) Certainly the only inn of the name in Britain, it replaces the *New* inn which has been in existence for over a hundred years. The new owner knows the island of Malta well and decided on *karozzin* which is a horse-drawn cab to be seen in Valetta, capital of Malta. A huge map of the island hangs above one of the inn's 13ft fireplaces.

Ketton Ox (Yarm, Co Durham) Commemorates the gigantic beast which became famous as the Durham ox. In 1802 when six years of age the animal weighed 34cwt and had a girth of over 11ft. There are many other signs including the *Durham Ox*.

Kicking Cuddy (Bowlees, Co Durham) A cuddy is a donkey.

Kicking Dickey (Dunmow, Essex) Dickey is the local name for a donkey. The excellent sign shows the donkey in fine fettle kicking a man and spilling his bucket.

King Coel (Colchester, Essex) Is identified with Cunobelin, the king who reigned over the area in the first century AD. King Coel is documented over many centuries while the Old King Cole of the nursery rhyme dates only from the seventeenth century.

King Ethelbert (Herne Bay, Kent) Almost every monarch and many other members of the Royal families through the centuries are remembered on inn signs, but Ethelbert the Saxon king who reigned 860-66 is probably the earliest. He was buried at Sherborne, Dorset.

King of Bohemia Usually associated with those signs referring to Christmas — *Three Wise Men, Three Kings*, etc. The *Queen of Bohemia* which honoured Elizabeth, daughter of James I, who married Frederick, Elector Palatine, for whom Bohemia was raised into a separate kingdom, no longer exists.

King of Denmark (Islington, London) In 1606 King Christian IV came to England to visit his brother-in-law James I. It is recorded that the two kings 'boused and caroused royally'. The name commemorates the visit.

King of Prussia Usually refers to Frederick II (the Great). Son of Sophia-Dorothea, daughter of George I, he reigned from 1740 to 1786 and was responsible for Prussia's paramount position in the German States. In the 1914-18 war many such signs were changed. At North Finchley, London, it became *King George V.*

King's Arms. Came about from loyalty to the Crown and many are very ancient inns. Some of the signs are well preserved and it is sometimes possible to gauge the real age of an inn and the coat of arms by the supporters or ciphers on the sign.

King's Head There are several hundred such signs which normally carry the portrait of a monarch. Henry VIII is the first in popularity, but the various Georges are also numerous. See also *Albert Edward.*

King's Wark (Leith, Scotland) Originally a military warehouse, it was later a royal residence. After having been almost destroyed by English invaders, part of it became an inn. Seamen all over the world refer to it affectionately as 'The Jungle'.

Labour in Vain Several of these are to be found. The signs usually show a coloured boy being bathed and scrubbed in an effort to make him white. There is a specially fine two-sided sign at Westergate (Sussex).

Islington, London N1

Lady Godiva (Coventry, Warwicks) The lady has been a legend since the thirteenth century, when she begged her husband to repeal certain taxes levied on the people of the area. He agreed on condition that she rode naked through the streets of Coventry on a horse. The ride has been re-enacted annually in Coventry since 1678.

Lamb & Flag Originally a religious sign, the sign represents the Holy Lamb with nimbus and banner. It was also the coat of arms of the Knights Templar. The original nine French knights bound themselves to protect pilgrims on their way to the Holy Land at the beginning of the twelfth century. Later the sign became the crest of the Merchant Tailors. The emblem was the crest of the House of Braganza and was also emblazoned on the standard of the 1st Tangier regiment commanded by Colonel Kirke, who became hated during the Monmouth rebellion. His men were dubbed with the bitter nickname Kirke's lambs.

Lambton Several inns of the name in the Durham area as John George Lambton (1792-1840) was a politician who later became the Earl of Durham. He was ambassador to St Petersburg, Berlin and Vienna and later governor-general of the British Provinces of North America.

Lambton Worm (Chester-le-Street, Co Durham) The name and sign perpetuate the legend of a monster worm caught in the river by young Lord Lambton. It grew to huge proportions and was eventually killed by him.

Lamprey (Gloucester) Lamprey pie was a royal delicacy in medieval times. They are similar to an eel in every respect, except that they have no proper mouth but attach themselves by suckers to other fish in order to feed off them. They are much sought after on the river Severn. The sign shows a lamprey, encircled by a crown.

Land o' Cakes (Manchester) This intriguing name for an inn comes from Robert Burns' writing on *The Late Captain Grose's Peregrinations through Scotland*. It starts: 'Hear Land o' Cakes and brither Scots . . .'

Land of Liberty (Chorley Wood, Herts) Perpetuates the fantastic story of the Chartist Fergus O'Connor, who in 1846 founded the National Land Company to buy estates and form a co-operative, the members of which would be settled on the land. Shares were 50 shillings each, which could be subscribed in amounts as small as a penny. At the outset, money flowed in and the first estate purchased was Herringsgate Farm, Rickmansworth (Herts). The poor people from the Midlands seized the opportunity of a new life and took possession of the land, but with their complete lack of agricultural knowledge and the stringent rules of the society enthusiasm soon waned. Eventually a select committee of the House of Commons looked into the scheme which was by then practically bankrupt. The company was wound up in 1851, and a year later the founder was declared insane. It was a group of disenchanted settlers who, glad of their new freedom, named the local inn *Land of Liberty, Peace & Plenty*.

Last (Church Aston, Salop) One of the many punning signs, comprises a man's hand

Axminster, Devon

holding a wooden last and around it the words: 'All this day I have sought for a good ale and now at The Last I have found it'.

Lathecleavers (Brighton, Sussex) Another of the old callings is remembered; lathecleavers were the men who split or cleaved lathes.

Leather Bottell The spelling varies from sign to sign but there are several with this name or derivations of it. Originally the sign of the bottlemakers company when drinking vessels were made of leather.

Le Chateau (Richmond, Yorks) Formerly the *Ship* it has recently been renamed. A feature of the place is a special wine dispenser.

Leckhampton (Cheltenham, Glos) The Devil's Chimney, part of the Leckhampton quarries, is featured on the sign. This rock pinnacle dominates the area and was probably left by the quarrymen as a memorial to their work.

Leefe Robinson (Bushey, Herts) Named after Captain W. L. Robinson who was awarded the Victoria Cross in World War I for shooting down the first German zeppelin in 1916.

Leg & Star Possibly came from the insignia of the Garter—highest order of knighthood in Great Britain and the world. Instituted by Edward III in 1348, the Order is limited to the Sovereign, members of the royal family, 25 knights and such foreign royalties as may be admitted. Each knight is allotted a stall in St George's Chapel, Windsor.

Letter B (Whittlesey, Cambs) The origin goes back many years when application was made for four licences. They were lettered A B C and D for convenience and licences were granted under the letters since the inns were as yet un-named. In the case of 'B' it has remained unchanged. The sign is a form of pun for it shows a boy with his arm round a girl from which comes the name *Let 'er B.*

Lima (Near Manchester) Takes its name from the capital city of Peru as it is situated in Peru Street. 'A "capital" house' as the brewers like to describe it.

Lincoln Imp (Lincoln) The sign figures the grotesque carving of the imp, a mischievous demon with long ears and only one leg, which is to be seen in the Angel Choir at Lincoln cathedral.

Lion First adopted as a device by Philip, Duke of Flanders, in 1164 the animal has figured on an amazing variety of signs. The lion rampant is the device of Scotland.

Little Wonder Several inns of this name in Yorkshire refer to the horse which won the Derby in 1840 at odds of 50 to 1, and originally cost his owner only 65 guineas.

Live & Let Live These are mostly to be found in the north of England. The name derives from the 'hungry forties', the term given to the period which preceded the repeal of the Corn Laws by Sir Robert Peel in 1846. Owing to the high price of food, there was distressing poverty among the poor.

C

Near Manchester

Long Sutton, Hampshire

London Inn

Lyme Regis, Dorset

London SW11—believed to be the longest pub name

retirement named it after the trow in which he had traded between the village of Llandoger on the river Wye and Welsh Back. Certainly it has a long and fascinating history with buccaneers, pirates and press gangs all playing their part. The book *Robinson Crusoe* evolved as a result of Daniel Defoe meeting Alexander Selkirk at the inn. Selkirk had been marooned on an island for four years and four months when he was rescued by Captain Woodes Rogers.

London Stone (Cannon St, London) Refers to the ancient relic ensconced in the wall of a nearby building. Some authorities believe it was a point from which the Romans measured all distances from the City; others believe it to be a Saxon ceremonial stone. Certainly it is London's oldest relic.

Lone Yachtsman (Plymouth, Devon) Named in honour of Sir Francis Chichester and Sir Alec Rose, both of whom set up transatlantic marine records. Chichester accomplished the fastest solo (east, west-southern) Atlantic crossing in 224 days in 1970. At Portsea, Portsmouth, is another *Lone Yachtsman* which commemorates Sir Alec Rose whose *Lively Lady* is pictured on the sign.

Long Arm & Short Arm (Lemsford, Herts) Situated just off the Great North Road it has access to two roads, one of which is long—the other short.

Lord Bexley (Bexley Heath, London) Nicholas Vansittart, first Baron Bexley (1766-1851) was Chancellor of the Exchequer 1812, a post he held for 11 years. Created Baron Bexley in 1823.

Livingstone (Birkenhead, Merseyside) The inn does not directly honour David Livingstone (1813-73) but takes its name from the street in which it is situated, named after the great African explorer and missionary. He discovered the Zambesi and the Victoria Falls.

Llandoger Trow (Bristol) This famous Bristol inn was built in 1664 and was originally one of five gabled houses. A Captain Hawkins who took the place on

Lord Clyde Popular, particularly in the north of England. Refers to Sir Colin Campbell (1792-1863) who was created a baron after his success in suppressing the Indian mutiny. Son of a Glasgow carpenter, he had a distinguished career serving in the Peninsular War and the Crimean War.

Lord Cornwallis (Tunbridge Wells, Kent) The inn honours the second baron who is Lord Lieutenant of Kent. The sign features his coat of arms.

Lord Eliot (Liskeard, Cornwall) Commemorates the English statesman, Sir John Eliot (1592-1632), who was born at Port Eliot, Cornwall. His policy of antagonism to Charles I led to his imprisonment in the Tower, where he died of consumption.

Lord High Admiral (Victoria, London) Lord Howard of Effingham (1536-1624) was the Lord High Admiral who commanded the English fleet against the Spanish Armada in 1588.

Lord Louis (Southampton, Hants) The inn was officially opened by Lord Louis Mountbatten and the sign carries his coat of arms. There is also a *Milford Haven* in Pembrokeshire which honours Prince Louis Mountbatten (1854-1921) who was an admiral of the fleet.

Lord Morrison of Lambeth (Lambeth, London) The politician Herbert Morrison (1888-1965) was born at Lambeth. He was created a life peer in 1959. The portrait on the sign especially features the quiff of hair so beloved by cartoonists of his day.

Lord Nelson There must be hundreds of inns named after Horatio Nelson (1758-1805) England's most famous admiral who entered the navy when twelve years of age and was killed in sight of his greatest victory at Trafalgar. Variations include *Nelson*, the *Hero*, etc.

Lord Palmerston Henry John Temple (1784-1865) statesman and twice Prime Minister in 1855 and 1859.

Lord Rodney The famous Admiral, who was a very popular figure in his day (1719-92). There are many variations including *Bold Rodney*, *Rodney's Head*, etc.

Lord Truro (Dalston, London) Recalls Thomas Wilde (1782-1855) who distinguished himself in his spirited defence of Queen Caroline. He was attorney-general in 1841 and 1846 and created Baron Truro in 1850.

Louis Kossuth (North London) The leader

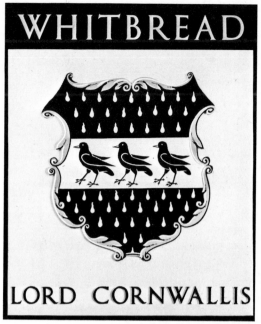

WHITBREAD

LORD CORNWALLIS

Tunbridge Wells, Kent

WHITBREAD

The Lord Morrison of Lambeth

Lambeth, London

of the Hungarian revolution who lived 1802-94. In 1851 he came to England, where he was received with sympathy and respect. In 1859 he tried unsuccessfully to inspire a rising against Austria. He also wrote a history of Hungary. See also *Independent*.

Lovers Leap (Stony Middleton, Derbys) The inn lies at the foot of a cliff over which, so legend has it, a young lady once jumped after a lovers' tiff. Her crinoline skirt, however, acted as a parachute and saved her life. The name of the inn was changed to record the event.

Lumbertubs (Northampton) Local greengrocers use of a field for the disposal of their vegetable boxes and other rubbish led to a nearby lane being nicknamed Lumbertubs Lane. The inn built on an adjoining site was the *Boothville* until changed to the present title in 1960.

Lumley (Maltby, Yorks) The sign is based on a drawing of Lumley castle in Co Durham, once owned by the earls of Scarborough. The inn stands on land originally owned by the family.

Mafeking Hero (Bishops Waltham, Hants) Refers to Lord Baden-Powell (1857-1941) who, during the Boer War, held Mafeking during a siege of 217 days by the Boers. When it was relieved on 17 May, 1900, the excitement in this country was immense and brought a new word into the English language —'maffick' meaning extravagant celebration of an event. Baden-Powell was also the founder of the Boy Scout movement.

Magpie & Stump (Old Bailey, London) The sign shows a magpie perched on a stump but the name is believed to have emanated from cockney slang. A magpie was a halfpenny and to stump up still means to pay up. In earlier days a half pint of ale was known as a magpie giving rise to another possible meaning.

Main Band (Bulgill, Cumbria) This describes a seam of coal in the Cumbrian coal mining area.

Mall (London W8) The sign depicts Charles II playing the game pall mall which was popular in the seventeenth century. A ball driven by a mallet was sent through an iron ring suspended on a post. From this the game of croquet originated.

Malta The island was recognised as British by the Congress of Vienna in 1814, which is probably why these inns were so named.

Man & Scythe (Bolton, Lancs) The sign shows a man with a scythe with the words 'now thus' inscribed on each side. The story tells of a man questioned about his mode of operation, demonstrating and explaining 'now thus, now thus'. An inn has occupied the site since 1251 and was rebuilt 1636; the Earl of Derby spent his last night there before execution for Royalist activities in 1651. A similar sign in Lancashire shows a man using a flail.

Man in Space The space era provided a theme for a whole new range of signs. The first satellite orbited the earth in 1957.

Man of Ross (Ross-on-Wye, Herefs) Commemorates John Kyrle (1637-1724) a local man who was a great philanthropist.

Man of Steel (Pontfaen, Mon) A tribute to the workers in the most modern steel plant of its kind in Europe which is near to the inn.

Manor of God Begot (Winchester, Hants) An allusion to its origin as a sanctuary when it was the property of St Swithin's monastery. Through the ages down to the Reformation, any person who had taken refuge in a sanctuary was secure from punishment— except for treason. The system was abolished in 1697.

Margaret Catchpole (Ipswich, Suffolk) This lady lived in the eighteenth century and her various adventures included stealing a horse which she rode to London, a distance of 70 miles, in 8½ hours. She was sentenced to death for stealing but transported to Australia with a life sentence. Eventually she married well.

Marlow Donkey (Marlow, Bucks) Takes the nickname of the diminutive engine which formerly hauled the local train from Marlow to Reading. The inn stands near the site of the former station. The sign shows the engine and a carriage used when the line was opened in 1897 and on the reverse side the type used in 1961.

Marquis of Anglesey Refers to Henry William Paget (1768-1854) first Marquis of Anglesey. A distinguished soldier, he commanded the British cavalry at Waterloo, at which battle he lost a leg. The leg was buried with his body when he died 39 years later.

Marquis of Granby Commemorates John Manners, Marquis of Granby (1721-70) a brilliant soldier. In 1760 during the Seven Years War he was in command of a brigade of cavalry with the army in Germany. Of his character it was said: 'brave to a fault, skilful, generous to profuseness, careful of his men and beloved by them'. After the wars, so the story goes, he set up numerous non-commissioned officers, who had served with him, in inns, which would certainly explain why there are so many inns bearing the name. It could also explain why, when he died aged 49, he left debts of £37,000. He was twelve times painted by Sir Joshua Reynolds, and some of the excellent signs are based on the portraits.

Marquis of Lorne (Wallsend, Tyne & Wear) John, second duke (1678-1743), who served with Marlborough; was a prime agent in bringing about the union with Scotland in 1707.

Marquis of Westminster (Belgrave Road, London) Robert Grosvenor, first Marquis of Westminster (1767-1845). Politician and art collector who laid out his estates with roads and squares, which now form Belgravia. He also fully developed the Pimlico area.

Martello (Folkestone, Kent) In 1804 when there was fear of an invasion, a number of towers were built off the channel ports as defence positions. Forty feet in height, they were of great strength. The name came from Mortella (Corsica) where there were similar

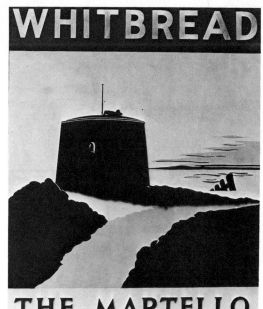

THE MARTELLO
Folkestone, Kent

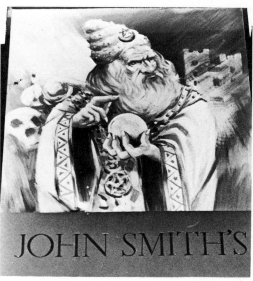

The Merlin, Andover, Hampshire

towers which had proved themselves in war.

Martyrs (Tolpuddle, Dorset) Commemorates the Tolpuddle martyrs, six agricultural labourers who tried to form a trade union in 1834. Regarded as a conspiracy in restraint of trade, they were transported to Australia but were pardoned two years later.

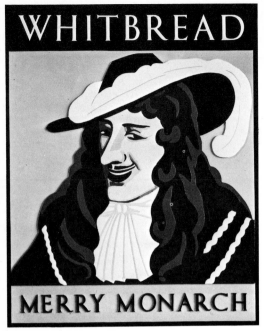

London N1

Avonmouth, Bristol

Mazeppa (Wednesbury, Staffs) Believed to have been the name given to a maze in the vicinity some centuries ago.

Memphis Belle (Kilburn, London) The name is believed to have come about as a compliment to some Americans who used to frequent the place.

Merlin (Andover, Hants) King Arthur's Way is one of the roads on a new housing estate where this inn stands.

Mermaid The legendary fabulous creature, half woman and half fish, was bound to be a popular sign at seaports. In Elizabethan plays the term was sometimes used for a courtesan. The *Mermaid* in Broad Street, London, was a meeting place for the great wits and scholars of the day in the seventeenth century.

Merrie Mouth (Fifield, Oxon) The sign depicts a large and merry mouth. The hamlet where the inn stands was named after the landowner—Fifield Murimuth. From this came merrie mouth.

Merry Monarch (London N1) The sign depicts Charles II who reigned from 1660 to 1685. The great plague of London (1665), the fire (1666) and numerous defeats at sea occurred during his reign. He was a weak but popular king. See also *Royal Oak* and *Rose Revived*.

Minden Rose (Bury St Edmunds, Suffolk). A reminder of the crushing defeat of the French at Minden, 1759, during the Seven Years War. The sign shows a rose surmounting men of the 12th Foot Regiment who fought with distinction at the battle.

Mint The one of the name at Exeter (Devon) commemorates the fact that 1000 years ago King Athelstan set up a mint for producing coinage in the city. Others of the name are said to be named from mints (the sweetmeat) which were very popular in the Restoration period. There is an *Old Mint* at Southam (Warwicks).

Mitre A religious sign based on the head-dress worn by bishops, it is especially to be found in cathedral cities.

Mitre & Keys A combination of two religious motifs—the bishop's mitre and the keys of St Peter.

Monkey House (Buckland, Hants) Once the *Crown* it was nevertheless always referred to as the Monkey House, after a licensee who kept such animals. This is now the real name of the inn.

Monkey Puzzle (Paddington, London) The sign shows an Araucaria, more commonly known as the monkey puzzle tree. A species brought from Chile in 1796 by Archibald Menzies, the botanist, gained its nickname from a remark that it would puzzle even a monkey to climb.

Monolulu (Hornsey, London) Named after the famous self-styled 'Prince Monolulu', a racing tipster who died in 1965. An Ethiopian by birth, his real name was Peter Charles McKay. The sign carries his likeness.

Monument (City of London) The inn stands near the Monument which commemorates the great fire of London in 1666. The column is 202ft high.

Moodkee (Malvern, Worcs) Named after the first battle of the war in which the Sikhs endeavoured to revoke the annexation by the British of the Punjab. The Sikh wars ended in 1849 when the Punjab was officially annexed.

Moonrakers To be found particularly in Wiltshire, where it is the collective nickname of the inhabitants. The legend recounts how a gang of smugglers using rakes to retrieve casks of brandy they had hidden in a pond, were stopped by Revenue men and asked what they were about. Pointing to the moon shining on the water the smugglers declared they were raking the cream off the cheese.

Moorcock An inn near Coverdale (Yorks) named after a locally bred racehorse, winner of the Richmond Gold Cup three times in succession.

Bradford, Yorkshire

Morris Dancers (Long Preston, Yorks) From the fifteenth century the morris dance was an integral part of English village life. The dancers usually represented characters from the tales of Robin Hood. Foreigners were portrayed by Moors or Moriscos. The custom came from Spain in the reign of Edward III and was originally a military dance of the Moors. Morris dancing remains a feature of the English countryside and is an exclusively masculine sphere—women are never included. The attire and style of dancing varies regionally.

Mortal Man (Troutbeck, Cumbria) The legend on this sign is self-explanatory:

Thou mortal man that liv'st by bread alone,
What is it makes thy nose so red?

Moses Gate (Bolton, Lancs) The inn takes its name from a district of Bolton and one traditional story of its derivation is that the keeper of one of the toll gates was a popular old fellow whose Christian name was Moses. Another possible though not so straight-forward explanation is that Moses was a corruption of mosses and gate from the Norse *gata*—an opening in the wall. Thus an opening in the wall to the boggy or 'moss' land. In Lancashire the name Moss survives in many places with names such as Kearsley Moss or Chat Moss.

Mother Huff Cap (Great Alne, Warwicks) 'Huff cap' is an old term for the froth on beer. In olden days the only way of judging the quality of beer was by its froth.

Mother Shipton (Knaresborough, Yorks) Named after a local witch and soothsayer, whose real name was Ursula Southiel (1488-1560). She compiled tracts foretelling great events. A small British moth is also named after her by reason of a resemblance to her profile on the marking of its wings.

Mount Radford (Exeter, Devon) Once a large country residence, now very much a built-up area. The house as it was 100 years ago is shown on the sign.

Mr Samuel Pepys (Upper Thames Street, London) This new riverside inn commemorates Samuel Pepys (1633-1703) the English Admiralty official and diarist. He came to prominence through the patronage of the Earl of Sandwich and rose rapidly in the naval service to become Secretary of the Admiralty. His famous diary ran from 1660 to 1669 when his eyesight failed. The period covered the great plague, the fire of London and the Dutch fleet sailing up the Thames.

Nag's Head Usually a humorous sign showing a woman wearing a muzzle, although sometimes just a horse's head is portrayed.

Napoleon There are several named after Napoleon Bonaparte (1769-1821) including those at Boscastle (Cornwall) so-named since 1807, Bradford (Yorks), Manchester and Guildford (Surrey)—an odd notion of the English to name an inn after a corporal who rose to become Emperor and a foreign despot, who in his day was more hated and feared than Hitler in our time. When levies were raised to repel the threatened French invasion the men had to report to the local innkeeper who was naturally dubbed 'Napoleon'—this could be a reason for the name. Things were generally evened up by the fact that wherever there was a *Napoleon*, there was invariably also a *Wellington*, the British general who finally defeated Napoleon at Waterloo.

Nautical William (Fern Green, Salop) Refers to William IV, sometimes known as the sailor king. For 21 years before his marriage to Queen Adelaide he lived with Mrs Jordan the actress by whom he had ten children. After his marriage he led an exemplary private life and was very popular.

Navigator To be found wherever there are canals, after the labourers who excavated them; the word became shortened to 'navvy'.

Nell Gwynne Refers to 'pretty witty Nell', mistress of Charles II. Though illiterate she was a good comedy actress, and Chelsea Hospital is said to have been founded at her instigation. She had one son by the king—the Duke of St Albans.

New There are hundreds of *New* inns up and down the country and most are something of a misnomer, for invariably they became 'New' inns when rebuilt, so that

WHITBREAD

MOUNT RADFORD

Exeter, Devon

certainly so far as their sites are concerned they are usually very old. One of the most famous of the name is in the city of Gloucester, where it has been in existence for over 500 years. Its story began with the foul murder of Edward II at Berkeley Castle in 1327 when, despite the danger, the Abbot of Gloucester bravely begged to be allowed to give the body burial in his church. A century passed, by which time the murdered man had become a martyred king and thousands of pilgrims made the journey from all parts of the country to pray at his shrine. It was in an effort to accommodate some of them that John Twyning, a monk, built the hostel in 1457—42 years before Columbus discovered America. The revenues from the pilgrim traffic over the years were immense and from them the abbey church was rebuilt to become the wonderful Gloucester cathedral that we know today. The inn still has its fine gallery surrounding the courtyard.

In the small village of Shebbear (North Devon) the *New Inn* was built in 1678 and has only in comparatively recent years changed the name to become the *Devil's Stone*.

New Broom (Rotherham, Yorks) The inn is on the Broom Valley estate where originally brooms grew in profusion. The sign shows brooms being sold to passers-by.

New Globe (Mile End Road, London) The sign shows a terrestrial globe of the world.

New Shovels (Blackpool, Lancs) It was built on the site of the *Shovels*, the name originating from the clay mining operations carried on nearly 100 years ago.

Nine Saxons (Nr Reading, Berks) Some years ago a Saxon burial ground was discovered in the vicinity and the skeletons of nine Saxons were recovered. The sign shows a Viking warrior surrounded by nine skulls. See also *Three Hills*.

Nineteenth Hundred (York) Commemorates the 1971 celebrations of the 1900 years since the building of York Minster, the largest Gothic church in England. On the site of a former church, building started in

NEW GLOBE

Mile End Road, London

19th Century Token
once used at this Inn

Worle, Somerset

the thirteenth century and extended well into the fifteenth century. The last major additions, the western towers, were finished in 1474.

Noah's Ark In 1864 there were at least seven so-named in London and today there are many all over the country. Originally it was considered a religious sign, for the deluge was one of the standard subjects of medieval dramatic plays.

Noble Art (London) Refers to the sport of boxing.

Norway (Perranarworthal, Cornwall) An inn has stood on the site by Restonguet creek for nearly 200 years, and in the early days was probably a beer-house to serve the men working at Perran wharf a short distance up-river, where ships from Norway discharged their cargoes of timber. For the return journey they loaded ore from the local copper mines. The inn sign shows a Norwegian longboat.

Odessa (Nr Tewkesbury, Glos) The inn sign shows ships of the English-French fleet bombarding the military port of Odessa on the Black Sea at the commencement of the Crimean War, April 1854.

Oily Johnnie's (Windscales, Cumbria) Formerly the *Royal Oak* this inn was re-named in memory of a former very popular licensee who, in addition to being an innkeeper, also 'peddled' paraffin round the district, where he was held in great affection.

Old Albion (Crantock, Cornwall) The name comes from a locally built ship. The sign, however, shows HMS *Albion*, a 90-gun ship that was built at Plymouth in 1842. *Albion*, always a popular name for a ship, was the mythological son of Neptune and Amphitrite.

Old Clink (Callington, Cornwall) A reminder that the old 'lock-up' built to accommodate two people stands opposite.

Old Mother Redcap (Blackburn, Lancs) In Elizabethan times there was a witch in the district whose presence always foretold disas-

Cheltenham, Gloucestershire

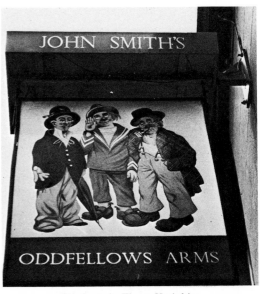

Sherburn-in-Elmet, Yorkshire

ter. Her spell could only be broken if she were encircled with a gold ring. The legend lives on in the name of the inn and the sign depicting a fierce old woman.

Old Parr's Head (Islington, London) Recalls Thomas Parr (1483-1635) who according to tradition lived for 152 years. A Shropshire farm hand, he married his first wife when 80, and his second when he was 120 years old. He did penance when he was 100 for having begotten an illegitimate child. He performed all his normal tasks until his 130th year and in his 152nd year was induced to travel to London to meet King Charles I and was entertained so royally that he died. The great physician, William Harvey, carried out an autopsy on him. He was buried in the transept of Westminster Abbey. See also *Henry Jenkins*.

Old Sergeant (Enfield, Middx) The sign is taken from a portrait of Sergeant Arthur Stevens, a Chelsea pensioner of the Seaforth Highlanders.

Old Success (Sennen Cove, Cornwall) An inn which by its name commemorates the joining of the Atlantic cables to the land lines for the telegraphic communication between America and London.

Old Welsh Harp (Nr Hendon, Middx) Is named after the Welsh Harp reservoir in the north-west suburbs of London. There is also an *Upper Welsh Harp* not far away at west Hendon.

One & All (Penzance, Cornwall) The motto of the Duchy of Cornwall.

One & Three (Oldham, Lancs) The number of the inn in the road is thirteen—one way of avoiding the 'unlucky' figure.

Orange Footman (Harlow New Town, Essex) Named after the moth, it has a handsome sign.

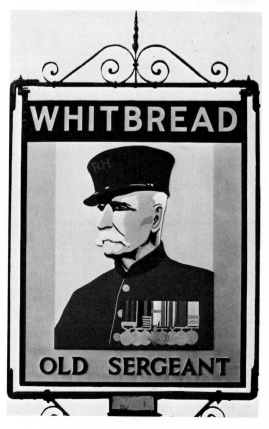

Old Sergeant, Enfield, Middlesex, based on a photograph of Sergeant Arthur Stevens

WHITBREAD

THE OLD COCK

Silver Grey Dorking

The oldest English breed dating from Roman times

Droitwich, Worcestershire

WHITBREAD

THE ORLANDO

Bognor Regis, Sussex

Bass

Old Thatched House

Shirley, Hampshire

Ordinary Fellow (Chatham, Kent) The sign carries a likeness of King George V and the title comes from the king's own words expressed in surprise when the crowds acclaimed him on the occasion of his jubilee: 'I am only an ordinary fellow.'

Orepool (Forest of Dean, Glos) The inn is situated in the centre of what was once the largest iron-ore mines in the country. The rich deposits were known as 'pools of ore'.

Orlando (Bognor Regis, Sussex) The name is the Italian form of Roland who, the legend has it, owned a wonderful ivory horn. He sounded it to give Charlemagne notice of his danger when he was set upon by the Gascons. A horn is depicted on the sign.

Our Mutual Friend (Stevenage, Herts) Is one of many taking the title of characters in the book of Charles Dickens *Our Mutual Friend* written in 1864-65.

Oxnoble (Manchester) This is named after a species of potato which was handled at the potato wharf at the nearby docks.

WHITBREAD

PACK HORSE

Mark, Somerset

WHITBREAD

PALACE

Leamington Spa, Warwickshire

WHITBREAD

PADDY'S GOOSE

Trealaw, Glamorgan

Pack of Cards (Combe Martin, Devon) This has been an inn for over 250 years and was built by an eccentric squire. The place resembles a house built of cards by a child.

Packhorse A popular name in the days when horses provided almost the only means of transporting goods. See also *Horse & Crook*.

Paddington Packet (Between Paddington and Uxbridge, Middx) Named after the barge service which was run on the Grand Union Canal.

Painted Lady (Harlow New Town, Essex) Yet another butterfly sign. On the reverse side is a 'lady of the town'.

Palace (Leamington Spa, Warwicks) The sign is rather splendid showing the Victoria Memorial with Buckingham Palace in the background.

Pandy (Tonypandy, Glam) *Pandy* is a Welsh name for a fulling mill. These were situated

THE PANDY

Tonypandy, Glamorgan

PAPERMAKERS ARMS

Tonbridge, Kent

close to streams which provided the power for the wooden hammers which continually pounded the cloth. The fascinating sign shows the process in operation.

Park (Tottenham, London N17) This is near the Tottenham Hotspurs football ground and is a new approach to a rather common name. The sign shows one of the trials of twentieth-century life—a parking meter with a post carrying the letter 'P'.

Parson & Clerk (Streetly, Staffs) From a longstanding feud between the local squire and the parson. In 1788, when this ended, two figures were installed on the roof of the inn representing the antagonists.

Passage House Quite numerous and usually to be found by a river or canal crossing; most of them are very old, some dating from Roman times.

Paul Jones (Whitehaven, Cumbria) He was the notorious and brilliant naval adventurer who lived 1747-92. Scottish by birth, he was a sailor, property owner in Virginia, saw service on a slaver and later with the American navy, when he raided the coast of Britain. He was commodore of a French squadron and as such captured two British warships. Before he died in Paris at the early age of 45 he was a rear admiral in the Russian navy.

Paul Pry (Peterborough, Northants) The hero of John Poole's comedy written in 1825, he was an idle meddlesome fellow who had no occupation of his own and was always interfering in other people's affairs. His name has become a synonym for lazy interfering persons.

Pavilion (Wormwood Scrubs, London) During the nineteenth century, grand military parades and reviews were held at Wormwood Scrubs and this inn is said to mark the site of what was on those occasions the 'Royal Pavilion'. The sign shows a marquee with an Indian orderly on guard.

Paxton's Head Named after Sir Joseph Paxton (1801-65) who designed the Crystal

Tottenham, London N17

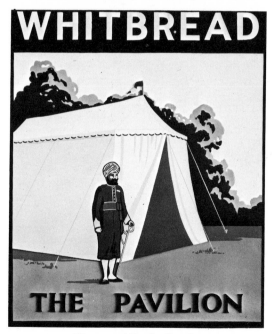

Wormwood Scrubs, London

Palace to house the International Exhibition of 1851. The Palace, one of the greatest achievements of the Victorian age, gave expression to the Industrial Revolution. Paxton thought out and completed his design in nine days after 233 other schemes had been rejected. The Palace was 600yds long by 400ft wide and covered 19 acres. Four thousand tons of glass were used in its construction. There are other inns commemorating the designer as *Sir Joseph Paxton*.

Peacock (Rowsley, Derbys) The inn was built in 1662 and was formerly the dower house of the Duke of Rutland whose seat, Haddon Hall, is nearby. The sign is derived from the badge of the family.

Pearly Queen (Stepney, London) The pearly kings and queens are a tradition of the true cockneys—those born within the sound of Bow Bells.

Peel Several of the name honour Sir Robert Peel (1788-1850) who made his mark early in politics and when Home Secretary re-organised the London police force. Both nicknames 'Peelers' and 'Bobbies' come from his name. In 1842 he imposed income tax at seven pence in the pound. He died after being thrown from his horse.

Pennycomequick (Plymouth, Devon) The sign is a facsimile of an 1865 penny, but the name is a derivation from an ancient local placename.

Pestle & Mortar (Wantage, Berks) Formerly a trade sign of the pharmacist; like many others it was copied for an inn sign.

Petre (Langho, Lancs) Takes the name from a family who owned lands in the area. Their coat of arms is shown on the sign.

Phantom Coach (Coventry, Warwicks) The inn is situated on the old coaching route and the story goes that a coach travelling between Birmingham and Coventry stopped near the inn and was never seen again.

Phoenix (Harlow New Town, Essex) An attractive sign depicts the Phoenix moth.

Coventry, Warwickshire

Regents Park, London

Burnham-on-Sea, Somerset

Picton (Newport, Mon) Named after Sir Thomas Picton (1758-1815) the famous soldier who achieved fame in the Peninsular War. He was killed by a musket ball at Waterloo when leading a charge.

Pier (Burnham-on-Sea, Som) The sign shows one of the pleasure steamers tied up at the pier.

Pig & Whistle A very old sign of which there are several still in existence. Believed to have been adapted from the Saxon *piggen*, a milking pail and wassail (be in health). When beer was served in pails and customers dipped their mugs in and served themselves, the mugs were called 'pigs'. 'Pige-washael'— the angel's salutation to the Virgin Mary meaning 'health to the maiden'—is another and very attractive theory as to its origin.

Pig of Lead To be found particularly in Derbyshire or wherever lead was mined. Pigs are the oblong ingots in which the lead was cast. They were formerly called sows.

Pike & Musket (Walton, Som) The inn is near the area where the battle of Sedgemoor

Bass

Pigeons

Curload, Somerset

Little Coxwell, Berkshire

The PLOUGH Inn

WEST COUNTRY

Bass

Pike & Musket

Walton, Somerset

was fought in 1685. A musketeer and a pike-man of the period are shown on the sign.

Piltdown Man (Nr Maresfield, Sussex) A permanent reminder of one of the greatest hoaxes of the century. It occurred in 1912 when Charles Dawson, a Sussex lawyer, claimed to have found cranial fragments of a caveman at Piltdown, which were of immense historical importance. For nearly 40 years they were accepted by anthropologists as genuine but eventually scientific tests proved them a fake.

Pindar of Wakefield (Grays Inn Road, London) A pindar was one who impounded stray cattle in the village pound. The mythical George-a-Green was the Pindar of Wakefield who resisted Robin Hood and his men when they attempted to commit a trespass in Wakefield.

Pit Pony (Easton, Bristol) A reminder of the work of the pit ponies in the coal mines.

Ploddy House (Taynton, Glos) Comes from *plodde*—a puddle, pool or swampy plot of land.

Walderslade, near Chatham, Kent

Plough A sign that is to be found in every agricultural district, for 'Plough Monday', the first Monday after the twelve days of the Christian festivities, was a very special occasion—the beginning of a new agricultural year. Decorated ploughs would be dragged in procession to raise 'plough money' for an ale frolic. On these occasions gentlemen feasted their farmers and they in turn their men. See also *Cornkist*.

Plume of Feathers See *Fleur-de-Lys*.

Plummet Line (Halifax, Yorks) An association with the building trade is the plumb or plummet line used in checking the perpendicular.

Poplar Kitten (Harlow New Town, Essex) Named after the butterfly and one of a series in Harlow.

Port Royal (Exeter, Devon) The sign shows the city basin with the warehouses in the background.

Bass

Plume of Feathers

Sherborne, Dorset

Pony & Trap

Chew Magna, Somerset

WHITBREAD

PORT ROYAL

Exeter, Devon

POTTER'S WHEEL

Hoyland, Yorkshire

Porter & Sorter (East Croydon, Surrey) The inn is situated nearby the Post Office sorting office and close also is East Croydon station. The sign has a different picture on each side.

Potter's Wheel (Hoyland, Yorks) There is a local historical connection with this name, for nearly a hundred years ago there stood near the site the Skiers Spring pottery then owned by Earl Fitzwilliam. The clay for the pottery was obtained locally.

Pride of the Valley (Churt, Surrey) The sign carries a portrait of David Lloyd George (1863-1945) the great Liberal politician who lived in Churt in his later years. As Chancellor of the Exchequer, a post he held for seven years, he was responsible for the Old Age Pensions Act of 1908. A pacifist until World War II, he became Minister of Munitions in 1915 and in 1916 succeeded Asquith as Prime Minister, a position he held until 1922. He became Lloyd George of Dwyfor (1st Earl) in the year of his death.

Prince Blutcher There are several which do honour to Blutcher, Prince of Wahistadt (1742-1819) the Prussian Field Marshal who aided Wellington's victory at Waterloo in 1815 by his timely appearance on the battle-field. He was then 73 years of age. He received the Freedom of the City in London in 1814.

Prince Leopold Usually commemorates the fourth and youngest son of Queen Victoria (1853-84). He was created Duke of Albany in 1881.

Prince of Orange Refers to William II of Orange (1626-50) whose son William III married Mary, eldest daughter of Charles I, and secured the throne of England in 1688.

Prinny's (Brighton, Sussex) There are numerous signs to the Prince Regent and George IV as he later became, but *Prinny's* is unique as it was a nickname given to him when Prince of Wales. Eldest son of George III he was born 1762 and died in 1830. He was Regent for ten years when his father was insane. He went through a form of marriage with Mrs Fitzherbert, the actress, but in 1795 married Caroline of Brunswick.

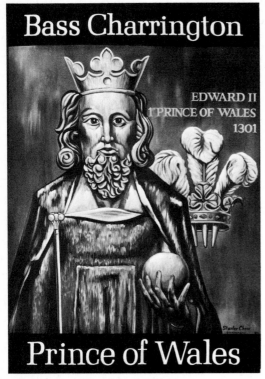

Dilton Marsh, Wiltshire

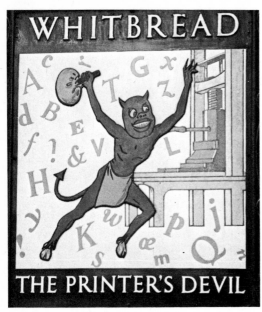

Fleet Street, London

Printer's Devil (London) The only inn so named is appropriately off Fleet Street. The name is given to a printer's apprentice.

Prospect of Whitby (Wapping, London) A famous inn by the river Thames, it is said to have taken the name from a three-masted vessel which plied from Yorkshire to London carrying coal and stone. In time the *Prospect* became well known at her moorings opposite the inn.

Punchbowl A sign that only made its appearance when the drinking of punch became fashionable. Punch was the Whig drink whilst the Tories preferred sack and claret. There is a *Punchbowl and Ladle* at Penelewey, Truro, Cornwall.

Purple Emperor (Harlow New Town, Essex) A further sign in the Harlow butterfly series.

Queen (London SW8) Refers to Queen Anne (1665-1714). Second daughter of James I she became Queen in 1702 and reigned for 12 years. She married George, Prince of Denmark, by whom she had 17 children, only 5 of whom survived childhood.

Queen Adelaide There are several signs to honour the consort of William IV.

Quicksilver Mail (West Coker, Som) The sign carries an excellent picture of the famous coach which became the fastest long-distance mail coach in the country. It maintained an average speed of $10\frac{1}{4}$ miles per hour between London and Devonport, and covered the 176 miles between London and Exeter in 16hr 34min, including all stops. It operated from 1835 until 1859.

Quiet Woman This has been a popular sign since the eighteenth century at least and believed at first to refer to Anne Boleyn, wife of Henry VIII. One signboard goes further with the verse:

> Here is a woman who has lost her head.
> She's quiet now—because d'ye see, she's dead.

The board of the inn at Earl Sterndale

WHITBREAD

QUANTOCK GATEWAY

Bridgwater, Somerset

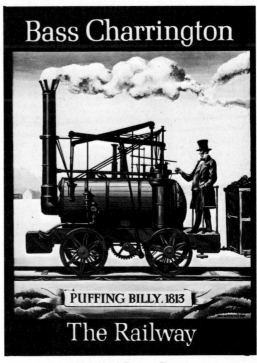

Bass Charrington

PUFFING BILLY. 1813

The Railway

Blandford Forum, Dorset

(Derbys) is surmounted by the words 'Soft words turneth away wrath'. Another variation of the sign is the *Silent Woman* near Dorchester (Dorset) or sometimes the *Good Woman*.

Rabbits (Stapleford Tawney, Essex) Said to be a corruption of the carpentry term 'rabbet'—a joint or a groove cut longitudinally.

Raglan Named after Lord Fitzroy James Henry (1788-1855) first Baron Raglan. A soldier, he fought in the Peninsular War and commanded the British troops in the Crimean War.

Rake (Littleborough, Lancs) The sign shows a nineteenth-century rake or libertine. The inn, on the old coach road over the Pennines, dates from 1696.

Ram Another common sign in clothmaking districts, as it is the crest of the Worshipful Company of Clothworkers. There is also *Ram's Head*. See also *Fleece*.

WHITBREAD

RAILWAY ARMS

Theydon Bois, Essex

Littleborough, Lancashire

Ram & Teazle The ram is, of course, associated with the wool trade. The teazle, a plant of the thistle family, was used to raise the nap of the cloth. See *Ram*.

Ram Jam (Stretton, Rutland) It is said that the title came from an officer of the Indian Army whose servant brought back a recipe for a popular drink—'Ram Jam'. The term was a native one for a table servant.

Rattlebone (Sherston, Wilts) A legend gives its name to the inn. It recalls the feat of arms of a doughty warrior, John Rattlebone, who fought the Danish invaders. He received a dreadful stomach wound but undaunted placed a tile against his wound to prevent his entrails gushing forth. He is shown doing just that on the intriguing sign.

Raven The bird was featured in the arms of Queen Mary I.

Red Cat (Greasby, Cheshire) In the local St Hugh's Chapel which was built in 1398, there is a sandstone corbel, often thought to have been intended to be a lion's head. It is known as the red cat from which the inn takes its name.

Red Dragon The red dragon usually refers to Wales, for it was featured in the early Tudor arms. See also *Dragon*.

Red Grouse (Stocksbridge, Yorks) A red grouse is shown on the sign in a traditional setting, copied from an old print.

Red Jackets (Camborne, Cornwall) Recalls the incidents when the miners created disturbances over the price of corn in the 1880s and troops were drafted in from Bodmin to quell them. The sign portrays a soldier in a red jacket outside the local market place.

Red Lion One of the more popular of the variety of signs which include the lion, it originally had heraldic connotations. Of the hundreds in the country, many probably had their beginnings from the badge of John of Gaunt, for some 30 years the most powerful figure in the realm. The *Red Lion* (Colchester, Essex) was built as a pilgrim's inn.

Red Rose The emblem of the Lancastrians, it is a popular sign.

Red Rover (Barnes, London) Named after one of the famous nineteenth-century coaches.

Rembrandt (Manchester) Honours the great Dutch painter (1606-69) whose preserved oil paintings total 650, plus 2000 drawings and 300 etchings.

Rest & Be Thankful A sign usually to be found at the end of a barren or very hilly stretch of country. It was meant to indicate a haven after a perilous and lonely journey.

Revenue (Devonport, Devon) An effective sign recalls the days when smuggling was prevalent in the area in the eighteenth century.

Richard Cobden (Cocking, Sussex) A great statesman known in his lifetime (1804-65) as the 'apostle of free trade', he was one of the founders of the Anti-Corn-Law League and became famous for the part he played in the repeal of the Corn Laws. Born at Midhurst, Sussex, a mile from the present inn, he was fourth of 11 children and spent 5 years at

Dotheboys Hall (of Charles Dickens fame).

Ring o' Bells There are a number of this name, which relate to handbell ringing—still a popular hobby. John Smiths Tadcaster Brewery ran a competition to find new inn signs and the sign was chosen first of 700 entries. See also *Bell*.

Rising Sun A popular sign which emanated from a badge of Edward III. See also *Sun* and *Rose & Crown*.

Rob Roy To be found in the Trossachs area of Scotland. Gaelic for 'Red Robert' the name comes from Sir Walter Scott's novel which was published in three volumes in 1818. Scott was a prolific writer, publishing some 64 titles, several like the *Life of Napoleon* running into three or more volumes. See also *St Ronan's Well*.

Robert de Mortain (Hastings, Sussex) Refers to the brother of William the Conqueror, reputedly the builder of Hastings Castle.

Ashcott, Somerset

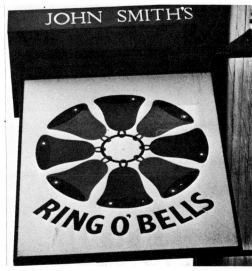

Barnsley, Yorkshire

Devonport, Devon

Rose & Crown Very numerous, the name symbolised the end of the Wars of the Roses, which had divided the country for over 20 years. Fourteen battles had been fought when peace came and then marriage brought the opposing factions together when Elizabeth of York, daughter of Edward IV, married Henry VII, and the inn signs celebrated the fact. See also *Sun*.

Rose & Portcullis The portcullis was a device of both Henry VII and Henry VIII and appeared in their badges. It is also the principle charge in the arms of the City of Westminster. It occurred on coins of Henry VIII and is used on the one penny piece of the new decimal coinage. The Tudor Rose also appears with the portcullis on this attractive sign.

Rose of Denmark (Poplar, London) Anne of Denmark who was the wife of James I of England—VI of Scotland.

Rose Revived A sign which became popular with the Restoration of the monarchy in 1660, after the years of the Commonwealth government.

Round of Beef (Cradley Heath, Staffs) Probably only meaning that refreshments may be obtained in addition to beer.

Round of Gras (Badsey, Worcs) The sign portrays a bundle of asparagus, for it is in the centre of an area where asparagus is grown for the markets. A 'round of gras' comprises thirty shoots.

Roundstone (East Preston, Sussex) In earlier days when superstition was rife it was the custom to bury witches, suicides and felons at the crossroads so that they could not be said to be buried within any parish boundary. To make doubly certain that the spirits of people so interred would not haunt the neighbourhood, a massive millstone was placed over the grave and a stake driven through the centre. This custom is faithfully portrayed on the inn sign.

Royal Blenheim (Oxford) Takes its name from one of the famous stage coaches.

Bass

Royal Mail

Taunton, Somerset

Royal Children (Nottingham) Legend says that the children of James II were playmates of the innkeeper's children.

Royal George (Worcester) Not one of the Hanoverians but named after the famous ship, built at Woolwich in 1756. She was 178 ft in length and 2047 tons. The ship foundered and was lost off Spithead when sailing to the relief of Gibraltar in 1782.

Royal Oak National rejoicing at the Restoration after the spartan days of the Commonwealth led *Royal Oak* to become very popular, for it was in an oak that Charles II hid at Boscobel (Salop) and escaped his pursuers after his army had been defeated at Worcester in 1651. Charles became a fugitive with a price of £1000 on his head. Imaginative innkeepers seized on the incident for their signs and the king is to be found in numerous attitudes hiding in a tree. Usually he is seen in full view. An attractive sign at Knockholt (Kent) shows oak leaves and acorns surmounted by a crown. The inn of the name at

New Inn Green (Kent) shows three crowns in the foliage of a tree, which represent the kingdoms of Great Britain, France and Ireland, which titles were claimed by the kings of England until the reign of George III. See also *Rose Revived*.

Royal Scot (Carlisle, Cumbria) This is the famous train which covers the journey from Euston to Glasgow daily. The train was so named in 1927. Until 1932, the journey time was $8\frac{1}{4}$ hrs; this was reduced to 7 hrs 10 mins in the post-war period and now, aided by electrical traction, the journey is completed in 5 hrs. The inn sign shows Bonnie Prince Charlie on one side and the *Royal Scot* of steam days on the other.

Rufus (New Forest) Named after William II, 'William Rufus' (1056-1100), third son of William the Conqueror. He was killed in the New Forest. See also *Sir Walter Tyrrell*.

Running Horses (Mickleham, Surrey) The sign records a dead heat in the Derby of 1828 between Cadland and The Colonel; the sign shows one of the horses on each side of the board. See also *Cadland*.

Running Pump (Catforth, Lancs) A pump is built into the front of the inn which bears the date 1834.

Ruperra (Cardiff, Glam) Refers to Ruperra Castle which is portrayed on the sign. It was the seat of the Morgan family.

Saints (Millbrook, Hants) Takes the nickname of the local football club.

St John of Jerusalem (London) The name comes from the hospital and church built in Jerusalem after the first crusade in 1099. The sick pilgrims were committed to the care of the Hospitallers of St John to whom the church was dedicated. A military order was introduced and when the Knights were finally forced to leave Jerusalem they went to Rhodes and later to Malta. The order is no longer a sovereign body but lives on as a nursing order for the relief of the suffering of the sick irrespective of race, class, colour or creed.

D

WHITBREAD

ROYAL MARINE

Combe Martin, Devon

WHITBREAD

RUPERRA

Cardiff

Exeter, Devon

St Peter's Finger (Lychett Minster, Dorset) Believed to originate through the mispronunciation of 'St Peter ad Vincula', a religious feast that was celebrated on 1 August in the nearby church.

St Ronan's Well (Innerleithen, Peeblesshire) Another inn taking its name from one of Sir Walter Scott's novels. A three-volume work, it was published in 1824.

St Tecla (Chepstow, Mon) The popular legend is that the saint was a recluse who lived on a small rock which can still be seen from the Severn bridge. She was supposed to have been ravaged by the Danes.

Salutation Originally a religious sign, derived from salutations to the Virgin Mary by the Angel Gabriel. During the Commonwealth it was unpopular and many so named were changed to *Soldier & Citizen*.

Saracen's Head In Roman times the name Saracen denoted any of the nomadic tribes

Chepstow, Monmouthshire

Topsham, Devon

that raided the Syrian borders of the Empire. In Britain during the Crusades it was applied to any Moslem or infidel. A great many ancient families whose members took part in a crusade included a saracen in their coat of arms. Another version of the sign was *Blackamoor's Head*. See also *Turk's Head*.

Saye & Sele (Broughton, Oxon) The inn sign carries the coat of arms of the family who have lived in nearby Broughton Castle for centuries.

Scarlet Pimpernel (Moseley, Birmingham) Baroness Orczy wrote several novels featuring a hero who had this pseudonym. A royalist partisan, he saved victims from the guillotine during the French Revolution.

Scutcher's Arms (Long Melford, Suffolk) One of the many inns whose name is associated with various trades or callings. To 'scutch' is to comb and loosen fibres by beating. It was a process used particularly for flax.

Sebastopol Numerous inns recall the great arsenal in the Crimea, which was put to siege by the British and French after ill-planned and ill-managed preparations.

Sedgemoor (Weston Zoyland, Som) The sign features the battle which took place locally nearly 300 years ago. The last battle fought on English soil, it was between the Duke of Monmouth's Protestant forces and the army of James II. Monmouth suffered a terrible defeat and was beheaded, whilst some 200 of his followers were either hanged or transported. There is a *Ye Olde Monmouth* at Lyme Regis, Dorset, where the Duke landed to begin his campaign.

Selsey Tram (Nr Chichester, Sussex) Commemorates the tramway which ran from Chichester to Selsey for many years until 1932.

Senlac (Battle, Sussex) Sometimes used as an alternative name for the Battle of Hastings, 1066, when William the Conqueror won his victory by taking the hill which the English were defending. The sign shows a Norman

Scarlet Pimpernel

Moseley, Birmingham

knight on his charger. See also *William the Conqueror*.

Seven Stars Popular religious sign of the Middle Ages. The sign represented the seven-starred celestial crown usual on figures of the Virgin Mary. Some signs show a constellation of stars.

Severn Trow (Stourport, Worcs) Named after the specially-built Stourport boats which carried goods from Stafford and Worcester down to Bristol via the River Severn.

Sexey's Arms (Wedmore, Som) In the sixteenth century a boy named Sexey rose to be one of the auditors of the Exchequer. Among other good works he founded a school and a hospital. The inn sign shows the benefactor as a boy and his coat of arms.

Shah Several of the name were in existence as far back as 1746, when they were named in honour of Thomas Nadir Shah or Kuli Khan, once chief of a band of robbers who eventually obtained the throne of Persia. He gained his popularity when he granted permission for the English to trade with Persia. A hundred years later the *Shah* at Huntingford (Herts) was so named when the Shah of Persia visited England in 1887. On this occasion he was much feted as his State was a buffer between the eastern aspirations of Russia and the Indian empire.

Shark (Harlow New Town, Essex) Takes its name from the moth, depicted on the sign.

Shaven Crown (Shipton-under-Wychwood, Oxon) The sign depicts a monk and recalls the association with the original Bruern Abbey. The inn was a pilgrims' hostel in the fourteenth century.

Sheaf & Sickle An agricultural sign, the sheaf of corn and a sickle—a reaping hook.

Sheaf of Arrows (Cranborne, Dorset) The sign is that of the Cecil family whose home, Cranborne Manor, is close by. The original house on the site is believed to have been built by King John as a hunting lodge early in the thirteenth century.

Sherlock Holmes (Charing Cross Road, London) Named after the fictitious detective created by Conan Doyle, the stories first appeared in 1891. Every year people of all nationalities call and sign the visitors book. The sign shows a portrait of the famous character.

Shiny Sheff (Sheffield, Yorks) An affectionate name given to the cruiser HMS *Sheffield*. When commissioned the ship's deck fittings and other gifts were presented by the City of Sheffield.

Ship & Shovel Sometimes said to be associated with Sir Cloudesley Shovel, the seventeenth-century admiral whose ship foundered off the Scilly Isles in 1707 and has in recent years yielded much treasure to divers. This theory, however, is far-fetched and is probably derived from the labourers who shovelled coal and ballast from ships and barges.

Shirehorses (York) Formerly the *Sea Horse*, the inn has been renamed because stables

Shakespeare Hotel

Plymouth, Devon

Shipton-under-Wychwood, Oxfordshire

have been brought into use since Samuel Smith of Tadcaster have recommenced deliveries of beer in the city of York by horse-drawn drays.

Short Blue (Barking, Essex) Recalls the fact that in the eighteenth century a fishing fleet known as the 'Short Blue Line' owned by a local family was based at Barking.

Shoulder of Mutton There are several of this name and it is generally thought to have been adopted as the name of an inn where the innkeeper had an additional trade of butchering. See also *Shoulder of Mutton & Cucumbers*.

Shoulder of Mutton & Cucumbers (Yapton, Sussex) The only inn with this distinctive name, which goes back some two centuries, when the cucumber sauce served at the inn was recognised as a Sussex delicacy. See also *Shoulder of Mutton*.

Showman (Cullompton, Devon) A changed name and sign to keep up with the times. The inn overlooks a field where a number of travelling showmen have their winter quarters. The sign depicts a showman endeavouring to convince a crowd of the authenticity of a two-headed dwarf.

Shrew Beshrewed (Hersden, Kent) The explanation is to be seen on the sign which depicts a housewife being subjected to punishment in the ducking stool. This was a stool or chair in which scolds were tied and plunged into water. Mentioned in the Domesday Book, the stool was in extensive use from the fifteenth to the eighteenth century.

Silent Whistle This title for several inns followed the railway closures of 1963 and 1965 under the so-called Beeching Axe. Richard (later Lord) Beeching was chairman of the British Railways Board responsible for the drastic reduction of non-profitable railway services.

Silver Arrow (Finsbury Park, London) The sign pictures the streamlined fast rail/air/rail route between London to Paris which

The Ship, Chard, Somerset

Cullompton, Devon

operates three times daily, the fastest taking only 4 hours. The locomotive appears on the sign.

Silver Ghost (Alvaston, Derbys) Refers to the Rolls-Royce car model which was in production from 1906 to 1925, the power unit being a 6-cylinder 7429cc unit developing 60 bhp. Some 6173 of the cars were made. The sign shows a Silver Ghost on one side and a ghost on the other.

Silver Oyster (Colchester, Essex) For hundreds of years Colchester has been famous for its oysters. The sign shows an oyster and a fishing smack.

Simon de Montfort (Leicester) Montfort, Earl of Leicester (1208-65), was the leader of the barons' revolt. He was the founder of the parliamentary system.

Sir Colin Campbell (North London) See *Lord Clyde*.

Sir Francis Drake Named after the great Devon seaman (1540-96). A thorn in the side of the Spaniards, he carried out a number of expeditions. Circumnavigated the globe and was knighted by Elizabeth I on his ship the *Golden Hind* at Deptford in 1581. See also *Golden Hind*.

Sir Isaac Newton (1642-1727) Takes its name from the man who discovered the law of gravity. He also invented the reflecting telescope and was elected President of the Royal Society in 1703, and was re-elected annually for the next 25 years.

Sir John Lawrence (New Southgate, London) John Mair (1811-79) was created a baron in 1869 after long service in India, of which he was governor-general in 1863.

Sir Joseph Paxton (Tichfield, Hants) Commemorates Sir Joseph Paxton (1801-65) who designed the Crystal Palace for the Great Exhibition of 1851, after 240 designs had been rejected. Built in the style of a giant conservatory, it was an entirely new conception in glass and iron. The building covered 19 acres of the 26 acres of the site.

WHITBREAD

Sir Colin Campbell

Gloucester

A million square feet of glass (4000 tons) were used in its construction. It was erected in six months by 2000 workmen. See also *Crystal Palace* and *Paxton's Head*.

Sir Richard Grenville The Elizabethan sailor who in 1591 fought a greatly superior Spanish fleet. His ship *Revenge* was in continuous combat for 15 hrs. His orders to blow up his ship were not obeyed and he was carried aboard an enemy ship where he died two days later. The episode was the subject of a poem *The Revenge* by Tennyson written in 1880. A fine sign with a portrait and the battle in the background is at Bideford, North Devon.

Sir Richard Steele (Chalk Farm, London) Recalls the essayist, dramatist and politician, who lived in the seventeenth-eighteenth centuries.

Sir Tatton Sykes (Wolverhampton, Staffs) Named after the famous racehorse, winner of the St Leger in 1846. The horse was named after the fourth baron (1772-1863), an enthusiastic racegoer who saw 74 St Leger's run. Until his last years the baron witnessed the Derby at Epsom annually, riding horseback from his home in Yorkshire.

Sir Walter Raleigh There are several which honour this great Elizabethan (1552-1618). He was born in a Devon farmhouse and rose to eminence at the Court. He was a soldier, sailor, adventurer and writer, his principal work being an incomplete *History of the World* written in 1614. He also is often erroneously credited with introducing tobacco to Britain.

Sir Walter Tyrrell (New Forest, Hants) Named after the man who reputedly killed William Rufus, in 1128. See also *Rufus*.

Sirloin (Hoghton, Lancs) The name comes from an association with nearby Hoghton Tower where King James I, when visiting in 1617, was said to be so delighted with the loin of beef served by his host that he knighted it—hence Sirloin. The oak table on which this occurred was the subject of a court action in 1969 when the trustees of the estate prevented it from going to the auction rooms.

Sixteen-String Jack (Theydon Bois, Essex) This was the nickname given to John Rann, a famous highwayman who was renowned for his grandiose way of life and love of clothes. He always wore sixteen silken strings at the knees of his breeches. At the age of 24 he had been on trial for his life six times but on each occasion was acquitted. Eventually he was again apprehended and in 1774 was hanged. He went to the gallows resplendent in a new pea green suit. Dr Johnson wrote 'Thomas Gray towered above the ordinary poet as Sixteen String Jack above the ordinary footpad'. The road near the inn is still known as Jack's Hill and he was reputed to have operated in Epping Forest. The very fine sign shows the highwayman on a cart beneath the gallows.

Slip (Much Marcle, Herefs) A miniature landslide or slip occurred near the inn during the sixteenth century.

Six Ringers, Felmersham, Bedfordshire

Theydon Bois, Essex

THE WONDER (LANDSLIP A.D. 1575)

SLIP TAVERN

Much Marcle, Herefordshire

THE SPA

Stonehouse, Gloucestershire

Slubbers To be found frequently in Lancashire and Yorkshire, a slub being a slightly twisted strand of fibre—the term is one used in the process of spinning and staining cloth.

Small Copper (Harlow New Town, Essex) One of the butterfly signs in the town is shown on the reverse side of a farthing coin.

Smoker (Cheshire) Perpetuates the white charger owned by Lord de Tabley who raised the Cheshire Yeomanry regiment in the Napoleonic war period. The horse had been bred as a racehorse by the Prince Regent. In the period 1790-93 it ran 19 races and won 12.

Snig's Foot (Ormskirk, Lancs) Gives rise to much speculation and is in the humorous category of signs. Snig is a Lancashire name for an eel and an eel, of course, has no feet.

Snowcat (Cambridge) Takes the name from the vehicle that was used with such success on the trans-Antarctic expedition headed by Sir Vivian Fuchs in 1957-58. Due in no small measure to the part played by the track vehicles made especially for the venture, Fuchs was the first man to traverse the Antarctic, covering 2200 miles in 90 days. He officially opened the inn which has a sign showing a profile of the snowcat.

Spade & Beckitt There are at least three inns of the name in Cambridgeshire and the Fens generally. It is believed that the beckitt may have been in the first instance a misspelling for 'becket', a tool that was designed for and used in peat digging in the fens.

Spanish Patriot (Lambeth, London) Received its name in honour of the famous Spanish Legion which, largely composed of Londoners, fought in the Spanish Civil War in 1936. Britain banned further volunteers in 1937.

Speech House (Forest of Dean, Glos) Originally built in 1676 as the Court House where justice was dispensed by the Verderers of the Forest of Dean, whose charter was granted in 1017. One of the rooms holds a famous four-poster bed so wide that no two ordinary men can shake hands across its expanse.

Spinner & Bergamot (Great Budworth, Ches) In days gone by the area supported a thriving weaving trade, so that the 'spinner' part of the name is obvious. Bergamot is a woven cloth comprising flock and hair and was first produced in Bergamo, Italy.

Square & Compass (Worth Matravers, Dorset) The name relates to the basic tools of the local stonemasons.

Star A religious sign in medieval days which referred to the star of Bethlehem. At Woodstock, Oxon, the sign shows three wise men from the east astride camels, being guided by the star to Bethlehem. There are variations including *Star in the East*.

Star & Waggon (Droitwich, Worcs) The very effective sign is a play on 'hitch your waggon to a star'.

Star of India (Nunhead, London) Sign is a replica of the British order of chivalry, the most Exalted Order of the Star of India. Instituted in 1861 by Queen Victoria, it was a reward for services in and for India and was used in recognising the loyalty of native rulers. The motto of the Order is 'Heaven's Light our Guide'.

Startled Saint (West Malling, Kent) The signboard of the inn bears the head of a saint, believed to be St Leonard, looking very concerned as an aeroplane flies around his head. The Royal Air Force station at Biggin Hill was a centre of air operations during World War II.

Stephan Langton (Friday Street, Surrey) The English theologian who became Archbishop of Canterbury in 1205. He sided with the barons against King John and was the first subscribing witness of Magna Carta. The sign carries his likeness.

Stepping Stones (Westhumble, Surrey) On an old pilgrim route, the stepping stones led the traveller across the river Humble.

STAR & WAGGON

Droitwich, Worcestershire

Stocks (Beanham, Berks) The sign shows the implement of punishment popular in bygone days for securely incapacitating persons for minor offences. They were secured by the ankles and served their period of punishment on the village green or near the church.

Stone & Faggot (Little Yeldham, Essex) In the mid-eighteenth century an alehouse was attached to the bakery. A fire of faggots heated the stones on which the bread was baked and when the place became an inn, it was so named.

Suffolk Punch (Ipswich, Suffolk) Named after the short thick-set carthorse of the county.

Sugarloaf Originally the trade sign of the grocer but copying by innkeepers was a common practice. The sign was often used in various combinations such as *Swan & Sugarloaf* or *Three Sugarloaves*.

Sumpter Horse (Walton le Dale, Lancs)

A name given to a baggage or pack horse. See also *Packhorse*.

Sun There are a number of the name, but of particular interest is the sign at Long Marston, Yorks, which shows the head of Edward IV and a sun image with white and red roses. Edward as a Yorkist king was very much involved in the Wars of the Roses, and was described as being very handsome. Before the battle of Mortimers Cross in 1461 due to a trick of the atmosphere three suns were seen.

Sun & Thirteen Cantons (Soho, London) A reference to the Protestant Cantons of Switzerland, and was named as a compliment to the numerous people of Swiss nationality who live in the district.

Swan Such signs are very numerous and have always been popular. Originally arose from the Order of the Swan, an order of knighthood instituted by Frederick II of Brandenburg in 1440. From this it was adopted by the Cleeves family and was used by Anne of Cleeves, fourth wife of Henry VIII. The badge was a silver swan surmounted by an image of the Virgin. In medieval times the swan was always accepted as the emblem of innocence.

Swan & Sugarloaf See *Sugarloaf*.

Swan Revived (Newport Pagnell, Bucks) Once the *Swan*, the inn was re-opened after a lapse and took its present name.

Swan With Two Necks A clear case of mispronunciation and ignorance, for it was originally the *Swan with two Nicks* and came from the annual swan-upping expeditions on the River Thames when the marks of the owners—the Crown and the Dyers' & Vintners' companies—are made. Royal swans are marked with five nicks and those of the companies with two. There is a *Swan with Two Nicks* on the Bridgewater Canal (Bollington, Cheshire).

Swingletree (Kellybrae, Cornwall) Takes its name from the crossbar to which a horse's traces are attached, which is illustrated on the sign.

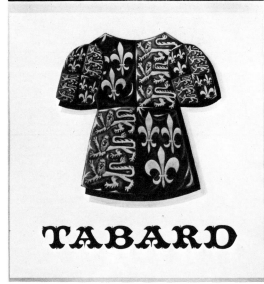

Hereford

Tabard The jacket with short pointed sleeves emblazoned with heraldic devices worn by military nobles over their armour, it is still worn by heralds. The *Tabard* inn from whence pilgrims set out for Canterbury was situated in Southwark, London and was immortalised in Chaucer's *Canterbury Tales*.

Talbot This was an old breed of hunting dog especially favoured too by packmen. The animal figures on several coats of arms including the Earls of Shrewsbury, from which doubtless many signs emanated. Always a popular sign, and quite a number remain.

Talma (London) Named after Francois Joseph Talma (1763-1826) the distinguished French tragedian. Was one of the first actors to make a point of accuracy in the costumes called for in the parts he was playing.

Tankard A drinking vessel which was in former days generally of silver and one of the most valuable assets of an inn. Silver tankards were once common in London inns, though often reserved for the more distinguished patrons.

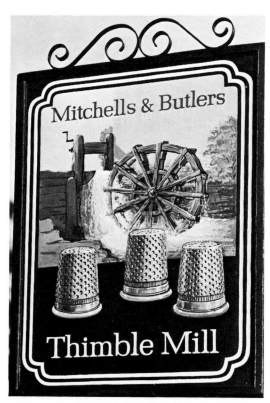

Waltham Cross, Hertfordshire

Smethwick, Staffordshire

Taxpayer (Copnor, Hants) Under the full title of *Jolly Taxpayer*, this must surely rank as the most humorous of all signs.

Teazle There are several of the name which refer to the plant used in pulling woollen cloth. The inn at Bromley, Kent, has a sign depicting a teazle.

Temple Bar (Waltham Cross, Herts) So named as close by is the Temple Bar which was formerly in the Strand, London. For centuries it was the principle gateway into the city and was used to display the heads of executed traitors. It was re-erected on this site when its removal became necessary because of street widening.

Thimble Mill (Smethwick, Staffs) A very fine sign shows three ordinary thimbles with a power watermill in the background. It came about however in error. The inn was built on the site of a mill which formerly manufactured spirit measures known as 'thimbles' to the trade. The name was the same but the appearance and use quite different.

1314 (Whins of Milton, Stirling) Situated close to the area where the battle of Bannockburn took place in 1314. Robert the Bruce with an army of 10,000 men annihilated the army of Edward II when the flower of British chivalry was killed.

This Ancient Boro' (Tenterden, Kent) Pays tribute to the long and picturesque history of Tenterden which received its charter in the reign of Henry VI. The town possesses all the privileges of the Cinque Ports. The sign is a reproduction of the Borough seal.

Thomas à Becket (London SE1) The English saint and martyr, son of a wealthy London merchant. He became Archbishop of Canterbury and his support of the Pope against the dictates of Henry II led to his murder in Canterbury Cathedral in 1170.

Thomas Cook (Leicester) Bears the name of the first man to organise a publicly advertised excursion train in England. Carrying

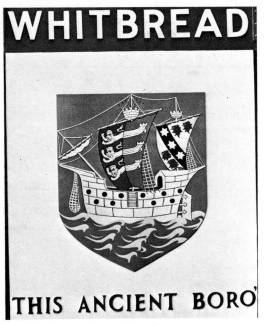

THIS ANCIENT BORO'

Tenterden, Kent

Three Tuns

Barnstaple, Devon

570 passengers, it ran from Leicester to Loughborough, the return fare being one shilling. Cook (1808-92) who had arranged the trip for a temperance society, was requested to plan others. The rapid growth of the tourist trade assured his success.

Thomas Lord (West Meon, Hants) He will ever be remembered as the founder of Lord's cricket ground, headquarters of the Marylebone Cricket Club (MCC) at St John's Wood, London. Lord (1755-1832) was also a famous ornithologist. His retirement was spent farming at West Meon.

Three Arrows (Boroughbridge, Yorks) The inn takes its name from the three monoliths close by which are known as the Devil's Arrows. The stones originally came from an area 15 miles distant and are thought to date from the Bronze Age, and were connected with pagan rituals.

Three Crowns Was a popular medieval sign as the three crowns signified the three kings who brought gold, frankincense and myrrh to the Holy Infant. Later signs carried a portrait of James I in addition to the crowns, thus identifying him as the first monarch to rule over the three United Kingdoms of England, Scotland and Wales. See also *Union*.

Three Hills (Bartlow, Cambs) Were three tumuli (Saxon burial mounds) found near the inn. See also *Nine Saxons*.

Three Horseshoes Usually represents the arms of the London Company of Farriers.

Three Sugarloaves See *Sugarloaf*.

Three Tuns Popular sign in days gone by. It was the arms of the Vintner's Company, which though incorporated in 1437 was known before that time. A tun, an enormous cask, contained 252 gallons of wine or 216 gallons of beer. See also *Half Butt*.

Three Willows (Birchanger, Essex) The most attractive sign shows three batsmen of different centuries, from the eighteenth until the present day, wielding the bat in real style. See also *Cricketers*.

Tigh-an-Truish (Clackan Seil, Argyllshire) The literal translation from Gaelic is 'House of the Trouser'. After the Jacobite rebellion of 1745, highland soldiers were forbidden to wear kilts whilst serving in the British army; a difficult situation, for when on leave at home they dare not face their own people wearing trews. The inn, therefore, became a cloakroom where they could change and honour was satisfied all round.

Tim Bobbin Several in Lancashire and the surrounding area which recall the fame achieved by John Collier (1708-86) as a Lancashire dialect poet. Tim Bobbin was the pseudonym under which he wrote. Son of a country parson, he was apprenticed as a weaver but turned his hand to many other things.

Tinker's Budget (Oswaldtwistle, Lancs) A budget was the small sack carried by a tinker containing food and stock-in-trade.

Tin Man's (Forest of Dean, Glos) A reminder that much mining was carried out in the district.

Toll Gate There are many so named, usually situated on or near sites where toll gates stood in the days when a toll was exacted for passing over certain thoroughfares. See also *Turnpike*.

Tom Cribb (London SW1) The English prizefighter (1781-1848). His first fight at the age of 24 lasted 76 rounds. As the 'Black Diamond' he fought Jem Belcher and Tom Molineaux to become champion, a title that was never wrested from him. The second fight with Molineaux in 1811 drew 20,000 people. With other prizefighters he was a guard at the coronation of George IV. Never beaten, he was allowed to keep his title for his lifetime. His integrity and sense of fair play made him a popular figure.

Tom Lock (Peterborough, Northants) Since 1290 there has been a spring known as Tom Lock's spring, at which the monks used to drink. The inn is close to it and takes its name.

Tom Thumb (Blaby, Leics) Named after

Bass Charrington

Toby Jug

Fareham, Hampshire

the dwarf hero of the nursery rhyme which has been popular since the sixteenth century.

Tommy Ducks (Manchester) The innkeeper, Tommy Ducksworth, employed a signwriter to repaint his sign, then the *Princes*, but wanted his own name included. The artist's letters were too large and he therefore only had space for Tommy Ducks. The name remained and is now the official name of the inn.

Tontine Several of this name exist in the British Isles. They were built by funds raised by a tontine, a form of annuity originated by a Neopolitan banker, who introduced it to France in 1653. The shares of those who died were added to the holdings of the survivors, until eventually the last survivor inherited all. As late as 1871, a London newspaper announced a proposed tontine to raise £50,000 to purchase the Alexandra Palace.

Top of the World (Warner's End, Herts) This commemorates the Mount Everest

Est 1659

TRUMPET

Pixley, Herefordshire

expedition of 1953 and the sign is based on a photograph of Sherpa Tensing standing on the summit.

Touch Down (Hartlepool, Co Durham) Associates itself with the adjoining rugby club ground.

Tournament Takes the name from one of London's superb annual shows—the Military Tournament held at nearby Olympia.

Trafalgar Bay (York) A reminder of the great sea victory in 1805 when Lord Nelson was killed. There are other variations of the event as inn names.

Traveller's Rest The meaning is obvious but the inn of the name on the summit of Kirkstone Pass (Cumbria) is 1300ft above sea level. There has been a building on the site for nearly 400 years, and it has been an inn for little over a 100 years.

Travelling Hen (Ponts Hill, Herefs) The intriguing name and the sign recalls the fact that a lorrydriver left the inn and on arrival at Birmingham discovered he had an un-invited passenger—a hen who had travelled the whole way on the back axle. On the return trip the bird rode with him in his cab, for which comfort the hen laid an egg before

the journey was completed. A little later the same hen 'jumped' another lift on the same lorry but to Cardiff. She again paid her way with an egg.

Treble Chance (Southmead, Bristol) An allusion to the football pools. The sign shows three horses ridden by three jockeys coming up to the winning post.

Treble Tile (West Bergholt, Essex) Nothing intriguing about this name, merely the fact that the inn and its predecessor are roofed with treble tiles—one of which is pictured on the sign.

Trip to Jerusalem (Nottingham) World famous and certainly one of Britain's oldest inns, for reference to it is made in old history books. Originally it was the brewhouse of the castle, which towers above. Then it became the *Pilgrim* and in 1189 took its present name. As the crusaders gathered to fight in the Holy Land they halted at the inn for refreshment. Its original spelling TRYPPE is an old English word for 'halt'. The inn is hewn out of the rock on which Nottingham castle is built, and is honeycombed with caves and passages. The whole place is unique and one of its chimneys of peculiar construction is only swept every 30 years, when part of a brick wall has to be demolished for the purpose. On the last occasion $7\frac{1}{2}$ tons of soot were removed.

Triple Plea There are several variations but that at Halesworth (Suffolk) has a sign depicting a man on his deathbed surrounded by a parson, doctor and lawyer, whilst lurking in the background is the devil armed with a trident. The generally accepted theory is that the three 'professionals' are arguing as to who has the greater claim to the body, while the devil bides his time to make his bid. See also *Four* and *Five Alls*.

Trusty Servant (Minstead, Hants) A very famous sign. The original painting by Hoskyns, a scholar elected in 1579, is at Winchester College. The basis is a symbolic figure, which combined the qualities considered in medieval times to make up the ideal servant for the college. The figure has a pig's snout padlocked, and so unable to betray secrets, the ears of an ass denoting patience, and a stag's feet to give him swiftness in the execution of errands.

Tunnel House (Nr Coates, Glos) Situated at one end of the 2½-mile Sapperton tunnel. It was part of the canal system built in 1783 to connect the Rivers Thames and Severn. Canal tunnels often had no towpath, so the horses were sent on overland. Men lay on their backs on boards and propelled the barges through, using their feet on the walls or roof of the tunnel, which often led to an occupational disease known as 'lighterman's bottom'. The inn was built as a hostel for the builders.

Turbinia (Newcastle-upon-Tyne) Commemorates the ship which was the first to be propelled by turbines. Charles Parsons (1854-1931) perfected the turbine for marine propulsion and, having failed to interest the Admiralty in his invention, made a dramatic appearance at the Spithead review in 1897. So successfully did his vessel manoeuvre that within two years the Admiralty adopted the invention. Parsons was knighted in 1911.

Turfcutters (East Boldre, Hants) Refers to an earlier local occupation when turf was cut in the vicinity for fuel.

Turk's Head The Exeter (Devon) inn of the name paid, in the thirteenth century, one penny a year to lean a beam against the Guildhall next door. In the seventeenth century the charge was raised to two pence. See also *Saracen's Head* and *Blackamoor's Head*.

Turnpike Quite numerous and a reminder of the seventeenth century when Turnpike Trusts were established. The system was that a body of trustees made up roads in exchange for the right to make a charge for all vehicles passing over them. There were hundreds of such trusts. At their zenith there were some 20,000 miles of turnpike roads controlled by 8000 toll gates. See also *Toll Gate*.

Turpin's Cave (Epping, Essex) This is one of a number of inns associated in some way or another with the infamous highwayman Dick

Turk's Head
Taunton, Somerset

Turpin (1705-39). Born at Hempstead, Essex, he was a housebreaker and robber but was hanged at York, 1739, for the murder of an Epping keeper. His legendary ride to York has no basis of fact.

Twa Dogs Taken from the title of Robert Burns' poem about the two dogs, Louth and Caesar. The former belonged in fact to Burns, whilst the imagined conversation between the two animals showed Caesar as owned by a wealthy landlord.

Twelve Knights (Margam, Glam) An historical sign. William the Conqueror appointed twelve knights to maintain order on the English/Welsh borders. They were paid for their services in gold and a reminder of this is a stretch of road nearby known as the 'golden mile'.

Twenty Churchwardens (Cockley Cley, Norfolk) The unique name comes from the ten parishes of a church group, each repre-

Canterbury, Kent

sixteenth century at work, dividing a curved tree trunk. Mounted on trestles and using a large frame saw, one man worked above and another below. It was by this method that the 'shaped' timbers were cut for the building of the naval warships of the period. See also *British Oak*.

Two Ships Recalls the encounter between the British frigate *Leopard* and the United States frigate *Chesapeake* in 1807.

Unicorn Once a popular sign with apothecaries, as the horn of the fabled beast was believed to be an antidote for all poisons. In medieval times it was believed that the only way to capture the beast was to place a maiden in his way, when he would lay his head on her lap. Supporters of the royal arms of Scotland are two unicorns. There are also several signs of the *Lion & Unicorn*.

Union Originally commemorated the union of England and Scotland in 1707. Later it also represented the union of Great Britain and Ireland in 1808. There is an excellent *Union* sign at Northleach (Glos). See also *Three Crowns*.

Van Gogh (Ramsgate, Kent) Named after the Dutch post-impressionist painter Vincent Willem (1853-90). He spent two months at Ramsgate when he was 23 years old as a teacher at a small private school for boys.

Vermuyden (Dutch River, Yorks) Refers to Sir Cornelius Vermuyden (1595-1683), a Dutch engineer who was given a grant by Charles I to drain Lincolnshire and Yorkshire marshes. The Dutch river, an artificial mouth of the river Don, was so named as a tribute to his skill.

Victory (Brendon St, London) The sign shows the most famous ship in British history, HMS *Victory*. Built in 1765, she was continually in service and was Nelson's flagship at the battle of Trafalgar, 1805. More than 300,000 cubic feet of timber was used in her construction. She carried 104 guns and a complement of over 700 officers and men. The ship is now permanently dry docked at Portsmouth. See also *Trafalgar Bay*.

sented by two churchwardens. At the inn each one of them has his own tankard engraved with his name and the parish he represents.

Twin Foxes (Stevenage, Herts) Recalls the famous twin brothers who were poachers. They were identical in appearance, a fact which when one or the other was appearing before the magistrates made for the confusion of the justices and heaven-sent opportunities for the defendants.

Twist & Cheese A twist is a roll or loaf made from twisted rolls of dough. The sign is indicative, therefore, of a drink with bread and cheese.

Two Chairmen (London WC) The chairmen were those who carried a sedan chair. This was a covered chair accommodating one person and borne on two poles. The mode of transport was introduced into England from Sedan, France, in 1634, and was very fashionable during the reigns of the early Georges, but disappeared when cabs were introduced.

Two Sawyers (Canterbury, Kent) There is a colourful sign showing two sawyers of the

Chard, Somerset

Volunteer A popular name usually recalling the old militia. The inn of the name at Exmouth (Devon) pictures a lifeboat at sea with a figure of one of the crew.

Von Alten (Chatham, Kent) A rarity but Graf von Alten (1764-1840) was a Hanoverian general who came to England in 1803. He entered the German Legion of the British Army and fought through the Peninsular War. He also commanded at Waterloo. On his return to Hanover he became Minister of War.

Wake (Nr Epping, Essex) Commemorates the Lincolnshire squire, Hereward the Wake, who held the Isle of Ely against William the Conqueror.

Walmesley (Billington, Lancs) Named after Sir Thomas Walmesley (1537-1612) who was born nearby and was a prominent judge.

Walpole (Blackburn, Lancs) Named after Robert Walpole (1676-1745) who became England's first Prime Minister. In the seventeenth century the title was Premier Minister.

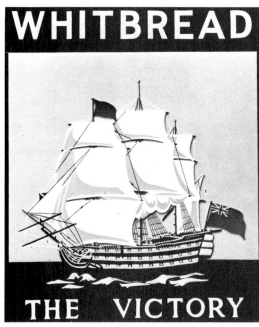

Brendon Street, London

Chatham, Kent

Ward Jackson (West Hartlepool, Co Durham) A local philanthropist (1806-80) he was chairman of the Hartlepool & Stockton Railway and responsible for building the harbour and dock. He was MP for Hartlepool.

Wash & Tope There are several of this name which originated from the fact that a traveller could wash or rest and refresh himself with a 'tope'—meaning to drink strong or spirituous liquors to excess. At Hunstanton (Norfolk) it was some years ago decided to give a new name to the formerly prosaic *Railway*, and a competition was organised to find one. The new sign is colourful and informative. It shows a map of the area and the Wash, on whose coastline the inn is situated. A tope is a species of small shark caught in the Wash.

Wat Tyler (Middlesborough, Yorks) Takes the name of the leader of the peasant revolt in 1381. After his initial success he went to Smithfield for a conference with Richard II. Wat was wounded, taken to hospital nearby and then removed and beheaded.

We Anchor in Hope Originally a religious derivation but the sign at Welling (Kent) shows the Pilgrim Fathers landing from the *Mayflower*. The first words they uttered on reaching dry land after their hazardous voyage have given their name to the inn.

Wheelbarrow (Southsea Common, Hants) Legend has it that the commander of Southsea castle was inclined to imbibe too well and had to be taken home each night by the innkeeper, who pushed him in a wheelbarrow. There is a *Wheelbarrow Castle* at Radford, Worcs.

Whiffler (Norwich, Norfolk) In earlier days a whiffler was one who took part in May Day revels and morris dancing. Later he led medieval ceremonies dressed in an imposing uniform.

Whistling Duck (Banwell, Som) Merely the result of a local newspaper competition to find a name for the inn. The suggestion of an eight-year-old girl was adopted. See also *Drunken Duck*.

Wheatsheaf

South Petherton, Somerset

Wellington

Bourton-on-the-Water, Gloucestershire

White Admiral (Harlow New Town, Essex) Named after the butterfly.

White Bear (Bedale, Yorks) As the sign shows, it is not one of the usual 'bear' signs, but a galleon built in 1564; it was one of Sir Francis Drake's squadron which attacked Cadiz in 1587.

White Boar Was a badge of the House of York, but when Richard III was defeated by Henry VII at the Battle of Bosworth, it was surprising how many *Boars* were repainted blue overnight, for that was the badge of the Earl of Oxford who supported Henry Tudor. The *Boar's Head* was also popular and such a sign dated 1668, which formerly hung in London, is preserved in the Guildhall Museum. See also *Blue Boar*.

White Hart A very popular and ancient sign used by Richard II as a badge. The animal is to be found pictured in a variety of poses. Legend has it that Alexander the Great captured a white stag and placed a collar of gold around its neck as often seen on signs.

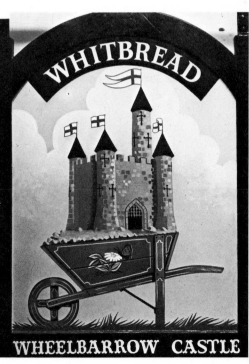

Radford, Worcestershire

White Horse This was the standard of the Saxons and the emblem of Kent. A galloping white horse was the device of the House of Hanover. Dickens used the *White Horse* inn at Ipswich in *Pickwick Papers*.

White Rock (Penycraig, Glam) The song of 'David of the White Rock' is a favourite in Wales. The sign depicts David playing a large harp.

Whittington (Pinner, Middx) Sign depicts Whittington with his cat. Other variations include *Whittington Cat*.

Who'd Have Thought It There are several inns of the name. In one Devon village the story goes that application was made for a licence and to the applicant's surprise it was granted—a fact he greeted with 'who'd have thought it' which the inn was duly named.

Whoop Hall (Nr Settle, Yorks) A name was required which would be associated with the local squire's pack of hounds and love of hunting. It was felt *Whoop* filled the purpose.

Bass Charrington

White Horse

Chard, Somerset

Bass Charrington

White Lion

Langport, Somerset

WHITBREAD

David of the WHITE ROCK

Penycraig, Glamorgan

Pinner, Middlesex

Bexleyheath, Kent

Redditch, Worcestershire

Why Not Sometimes a humorous meaning for this name, but that at Redditch (Worcs) shows the famous racehorse which won the Grand National in 1894.

Widow's Son (Bow, London) Named from the sad story of a boy who went to sea and never returned.

Wig & Fidgett (Boxsted, Essex) The words are believed to stem from old English words— wig-whicken, an old form for white, and fitchet, a polecat, thus white polecat.

William Camden (Bexleyheath, Kent) Great scholar, cleric, antiquary and historian (1551-1623). His greatest work was the survey of the British Isles, *Britannia*, published in 1586. His other works included the *Trial of the Gunpowder Plot Conspirators*.

William Dighton (Halifax, Yorks) Carries the name of the Customs & Excise officer who was responsible for the smashing of the infamous eighteenth-century Cragg Vale coining gang.

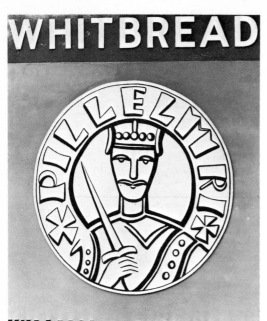

WILLIAM THE CONQUEROR
Rye Harbour, Sussex

WILLIAM WILBERFORCE
East Farleigh, Kent

William the Conqueror (Rye Harbour, Sussex) Invaded England and was crowned king in 1066. The sign is based on a silver penny of the period. See also *Senlac*.

William Wilberforce (East Farleigh, Kent) The sign bears a portrait of William Wilberforce (1759-1833) the great philanthropist who was the leader in the cause of the abolition of slavery. His bill was four times defeated in Parliament but eventually carried in 1807, after a campaign lasting 19 years.

Willow Beauty (Harlow New Town, Essex) One of the many signs which are named after butterflies and moths.

Woodin's Shades (Bishopsgate, London) In 1863 William Woodin, a beer retailer, owned the place and gave it his name which has been retained ever since.

Woolpack In medieval times wherever there were great sheep walks, so there were many inns of this name. See also *Fleece, Ram, Golden Fleece*.

Woolwich Infant (Woolwich, London) The name was given to what was in 1870 the largest gun made in England. Weighing 35 tons and designed for turret ships, it was the forerunner of heavier guns. In 1887, a gun weighing 111 tons designed for land use was made and was at that time the largest gun in existence.

World's End Several of this name, the most famous being at Knaresborough (Yorks). Stems from a prediction by the seventeenth-century local soothsayer, Mother Shipton, who foretold that when the bridge fell for a third time it would be the end of the world. Often an inn of this name was on the border of one or more parishes. An inn of the name at Almer, near Blandford (Dorset) dates from 1589. Field Marshal Montgomery stayed there in 1942 when planning the Normandy invasion in World War II.

XL (Garstang, Lancs) The two letters on the sign are an abbreviation of excel.

Ye Olde Tippling Philosopher (Caldicot,

Mon) Of many theories advanced, the most likely is that it was originally owned by a local man named Tippling (still a name frequently found in the area). It could of course stem from the dictionary definition of a house that sold liquor in small quantities—'a tippling house'.

York Minster (Soho, London) Its name derives from the fact that it was once church property. Some 75 years ago a licence was granted to sell spirits etc to a Frenchman—the first ever to obtain such a licence in London; the inn therefore also bears the nickname *French House*.

Yorker (Piccadilly, London) Commemorates William Gilbert Grace (1848-1915). Born near Bristol he obtained his medical degree in 1879 and took up a practice at Bristol. It was however as a cricketer that he became famous. Twice he captained the English team and toured Canada, USA and Australia. Though a superb all-rounder he was supreme as a batsman and in 1876 scored 400 runs not out. By 1895 he had scored 100 centuries and in his 43 years of cricket made 126 centuries and scored 54,896 runs. The portrait on the sign is based on the famous 'Spy' cartoon.

Young Vanish (Glapwell, Derbys) Takes its name like so many others in the north country from a famous racehorse who reigned supreme from 1823 to 1832. The sign carries a picture of the horse copied from a painting by John F. Herring, the great animal painter; formerly a stage-coach driver, he became famous for his animal studies.

Yutick's Nest (Blackburn, Lancs) In 1875 the old established inn was renamed by the new licensee, who was a 'drawer-in' at the local mills. His work consisted of threading a beam through reeds before fitting it to a loom for weaving. The 'utick' or 'yutick' was the old Lancashire name for a whinchat which builds its nest on the ground and spends much time over it, in what appears to be a sitting posture. The 'drawers-in' crouched over low stools for their work and so in course of time the men who did the work became known as 'yuticks'.

Bass

Windmill

Gloucester

Windwhistle Inn

Chard, Somerset

Acknowledgements

The author wishes to offer his sincere thanks and appreciation to all who have supplied information for this book. The collection of the material has been spread over a number of years and innumerable people have been of help in various ways.

Especially appreciated has been the assistance and courtesy of the brewery companies. They include:
Bass Charrington Ltd, Birmingham
Berni Inns Ltd, Bristol
Courage (Eastern) Brewery, Horsleydown, London SE1
Devenish Redruth Brewery Ltd, Redruth, Cornwall
Ind-Coope Ltd, Burton-on-Trent, Staffordshire
Mitchells & Butlers Ltd, Cape Hill Brewery, Birmingham
Rayment & Co Ltd, Buntingford, Hertfordshire
Frederic Robinson Ltd, Stockport, Cheshire
John Smith's Tadcaster Brewery Ltd, Tadcaster, Yorkshire
Samuel Smith, Old Brewery (Tadcaster) Ltd, Tadcaster, Yorkshire
Daniel Thwaites & Co Ltd, Star Brewery, Blackburn, Lancashire
Trust Houses Ltd, London
Watney Mann Ltd, London SW1
Charles Wells Ltd, The Brewery, Bedford, Bedfordshire
Thomas Wethered & Sons Ltd, Marlow, Buckinghamshire
Whitbread & Co Ltd, Chiswell Street, London EC1
Whitbread East Pennines Ltd, Sheffield, Yorkshire
Whitbread Flowers Ltd, Cheltenham, Gloucestershire
Whitbread Fremlin Ltd, Maidstone, Kent
Whitbread Wales Ltd, Cardiff, Glamorganshire
Whitbread Wessex Ltd, Romsey, Hampshire
Whitbread West Pennines Ltd, Blackburn, Lancashire

The author's thanks are also extended to Messrs Stanley Chew of Buckfastleigh (Devon) and John 'Rembrandt' Cook, sign artists, to Librarians everywhere and to a host of PRO's, managers and licensees.